"*This is a full banquet, rich in Bible truths, of personal anecdotes written with the forceful, penetrating language of instruction and exhortation.*"

<u>**Christian Review**</u>

"*Discipline is the wholehearted yes to the call of God. When I know myself called, summoned, addressed, taken possession of, known, acted upon, I have heard the Master. I put myself gladly, fully, and forever at His disposal, and to whatever He says my answer is yes.*"

In *Discipline: The Glad Surrender*, **Elisabeth Elliot** reminds you that you serve a loving, merciful God who allows you the freedom to *choose* to obey His call. She shows you how to commit yourself to Jesus Christ daily as you submit willfully and joyfully to His commands.

Elisabeth Elliot

Discipline

The Glad Surrender

Fleming H. Revell
A Division of Baker Book House
Grand Rapids, Michigan 49506

Quotation from "Ash Wednesday" in THE WASTE LAND AND OTHER POEMS by T. S. Eliot. Reprinted by permission of Harcourt Brace Jovanovich, Inc.

Scripture quotations identified KJV are from the King James Version of the Bible.

Scripture quotations identified RSV are from the Revised Standard Version of the Bible, copyrighted 1946, 1952, © 1971 and 1973.

Scripture quotations identified JERUSALEM are from The Jerusalem Bible, copyright © 1966 by Darton, Longman & Todd, Ltd. and Doubleday and Company, Inc. Used by permission of the publishers.

Scripture quotations identified PHILLIPS are from THE NEW TESTAMENT IN MODERN ENGLISH (Revised Edition), translated by J. B. Phillips. © J. B. Phillips 1958, 1960, 1972. Used by permission of Macmillan Publishing Co., Inc.

Scripture quotations identified YOUNG CHURCHES are from LETTERS TO YOUNG CHURCHES by J. B. Phillips. Copyright © 1947, 1957 by Macmillan Publishing Co., Inc., renewed 1975 by J. B. Phillips. Copyright © 1968 by J. B. Phillips. Used by permission.

Scripture quotations identified NEB are from the New English Bible. © The Delegates of the Oxford University Press and the Syndics of the Cambridge University Press 1961, 1970. Reprinted by permission.

Quotation from TOWARD JERUSALEM by Amy Carmichael taken from copyrighted material and used by permission of the Christian Literature Crusade, Fort Washington, Pa. 19034.

Library of Congress Cataloging in Publication Data
Elliot, Elisabeth.
Discipline, the glad surrender.

1. Christian life—1960–   . I. Title.
BV4501.2.E364   1982   248.4   82-9031
ISBN 0-8007-1318-4   AACR2
ISBN 0-8007-5195-7 (pbk)

Fifteenth printing, January 1993

Printed in the United States of America

Strive to choose, not that which is easiest, but that which is most difficult. Do not deprive your soul of the agility which it needs to mount up to Him.

SAINT JOHN OF THE CROSS

Contents

Discipline
The Glad Surrender

ONE

Created, Cared for, Called

EARLY IN THE MORNING I sit on a window seat in a beautiful stone cottage on a remote hilltop in south Texas. It is spring-time. There is no telephone or television and no human being within sight or sound, except my husband, Lars, who is reading up in the loft. The silence is total, except for the chatter of squirrels and the calls of birds—cardinals, scrub jays, a house finch, a wild turkey and a black-crested titmouse—some of which have allowed us to see them at the feeder or have given us glimpses as they flash through the live oaks and gnarled junipers that completely surround us.

Out from the shadowed grove of trees comes a solitary ewe. She walks delicately among sharp stones, nibbling sparse new grass, not minding the gentle rain, which is easily shed by her oiled wool. Is she lost? Where is the rest of the flock? She seems to be at peace. After a short time she disappears over the ridge.

Next a little wild pig, a javelina, comes. He snuffles the ground, finding tidbits here and there, even among these rocks. I notice that he limps slightly, favoring the left front hoof, which seems to be swollen. Suddenly he lifts his button nose, tipping it like a radar-scanning saucer toward the bird feeder, from which he receives tidings of something edible. He trembles for a moment, sniffing ecstatically, then springs from the ground in a neat arc, but not nearly high enough, not even close to the feeder. Landing painfully on the hurt foot, he makes no sound of complaint and zigzags off into the trees again. I wish I could bind up the hoof, comfort him somehow. That is beyond my powers, but I have recourse to another kind of succor, better than any bandage. I pray for him. "Here is your pig, Lord. Please heal his foot." It is possible that he was brought to my window this morning (the javelina is normally a timid nocturnal creature) precisely in order to be prayed for.

The closer one comes to the center of things, the better able he is to observe the connections. Everything created is connected, for everything is produced by the same mind, the same love, and is dependent on the same Creator. He who masterminded the universe, the Lord God Omnipotent, is the One who called the stars into being, commanded light, spoke the Word that brought about the existence of time and space and every form of matter: salt and stone, rose and redwood, feather and fur and fin and flesh. The titmouse and the turkey answer to Him. The sheep, the pig, and the finch are His, at His disposal, possessed and known by Him.

We too are created, owned, possessed, known. We are dependent as the javelina is dependent. As I look at the ewe, peaceful, dependent, finding her food provided by the Lord, I think of how He provides for me as well.

My father was an amateur ornithologist who, as a young man, had taken an interest in birds long before bird-watching became a popular pastime. He would walk in the woods and imitate the calls and songs of birds, often drawing them near, in the branches over his head. He gave lectures, illustrated with colored slides, in which he talked about the habits of the birds and beautifully imitated their songs. He nearly always closed his lecture with these lines:

> Said the Robin to the Sparrow,
> "I should really like to know
> Why these anxious human beings
> Rush about and worry so."
>
> Said the Sparrow to the Robin,
> "Friend, I think that it must be
> That they have no heavenly Father
> Such as cares for you and me."

Have we no such loving Father? We have, of course.

... Thou hast made all by thy wisdom; and the earth is full of thy creatures.... All of them look expectantly to thee to give them their food at the proper time; what thou givest them they gather up.... when thou takest away their breath, they fail ... but when thou breathest into them, they recover....

Cast all your cares on him, for you are his charge.

Look at the birds of the air; they do not sow and reap and store in barns, yet your heavenly Father feeds them. You are worth more than the birds!

* * * *

I am back home in Massachusetts now.

Last evening as the sun went down a thick fog rolled in off the sea. I could see the dim shapes of the sea gulls in the midst of it, winging their way unerringly west to Kettle Island, where they roost at night, guided by what the world calls "instinct," which is probably scientists' way of saying that they have no idea what guides them. I believe God guides them. Are they aware of it? Do the robin and the sparrow know they are cared for? We do not know. We do know there is a profound difference between them and us.

We say "free as a bird," but the truth is God meant us to

be freer than birds. He made us in His own image, which means He gave us things He did not give them: reason and will and the power to choose.

God calls me. In a deeper sense than any other species of earthbound creature, I am called. And in a deeper sense I am free, for I can ignore the call. I can turn a deaf ear. I can say that no call came. I can deny that God called or even that God exists. What a gift of amazing grace—that the One who made me allows me to deny His existence! God created me with the power to disobey, for the freedom to obey would be nothing at all without the corresponding freedom to disobey. I can answer no, or I can answer yes. My fulfillment as a human being depends on my answer, for it is a loving Lord who calls me through the world's fog to His island of peace. If I trust Him, I will obey Him gladly.

TWO

Discipline: The Answer to God's Call

No STORY in the Bible captured me more powerfully, when I was a child, than the story of the prophet Eli and the boy Samuel. It was in the time when "... the word of the Lord was seldom heard, and no vision was granted.... Samuel had not yet come to know the Lord, and the word of the Lord had not been disclosed to him." The child was sleeping alone in the temple, near the Ark of God, when he heard what he thought was Eli's voice calling his name. Three times he ran obediently to his master; three times he was told that Eli had not called. At last the old prophet realized that it was the Lord and told the boy what to say next time.

"The Lord came and stood there, and called, 'Samuel, Samuel,' as before. Samuel answered, 'Speak; thy servant hears thee.'"

I believed, when I was very small, that if the Lord could call the boy Samuel, He could call me. I often said to Him, "Speak, Lord," hoping that He would come and stand as He had beside Samuel. Of course I hoped for an audible voice, a light in the room, the hand of the Lord laid palpably on mine. The Lord did not grant that kind of answer, but His Word came to me nevertheless, in a thousand ways, beginning with the faithful Bible teaching my parents gave me and continuing through the years, line upon line, precept upon precept, here a little and there a little.

There is, in the great biographies of the Bible, always the

sense of men being confronted by God. The Bible is, in fact, a book about God and men—God knowing and calling men, men responding to and knowing God.

God blessed Adam and Eve and gave them responsibility immediately, to be fruitful, to rule the earth and everything in it. There were several exchanges between God and Adam before he and Eve decided to disobey Him. When they did, even though eating the forbidden fruit was Eve's idea, it was Adam who was summoned: "Where are you?" Adam made excuses for himself, but God continued to address him—by questioning: "Who told you?" "Have you eaten?" "What have you done?" God required response, for He had made a creature who was responsible.

God confided in Noah His plan to destroy the earth. He told Noah how he and his family could escape the judgment—if they would obey. "But with you I will make a covenant. . . . Exactly as God had commanded him, so Noah did."

Abraham was chosen to be the "father of many nations." Strict obedience was asked of him, obedience that would entail sacrifice from a seventy-five-year-old man: separation from everything that had been familiar to him, uprooting from comfortable surroundings, relinquishing of possessions and material security. But he ". . . set out as the Lord had bidden him. . . ."

Moses was another one. There could be no doubt in his mind that he was being divinely summoned when a voice (perhaps the first voice he had heard for a long time—he was far off in the wilderness, minding sheep) spoke his name out of a bush that was on fire. Moses responded. "Yes, here I am."

In the lives of Samuel, David, Jeremiah, Matthew, and Saul of Tarsus, as well as in many others in the Bible, there is evident the strong sense of being known, of being taken over, possessed, called, acted upon. They were not men who were especially concerned with the questions Is God using me? How can I be a great servant of God? They were not concerned with credit, with plans for notoriety or success. Whatever their own plans might have been, God's took precedence.

As a child in a Christian home, I did not start out with an understanding of the word *discipline*. I simply knew that I belonged to people who loved me and cared for me. That is dependence. They spoke to me, and I answered. That is responsibility. They gave me things to do, and I did them. That is obedience. It adds up to discipline. In other words, the totality of the believer's response is discipline. While there are instances where the two words *discipline* and *obedience* seem to be interchangeable, I am using the first as comprehending the second and always presupposing both dependence and responsibility. We might say that *discipline* is the disciple's "career." It defines the very shape of the disciple's life. *Obedience,* on the other hand, refers to specific action.

Discipline is the believer's answer to God's call. It is the recognition, not of the solution to his problems or the supply of his needs, but of *mastery.* God addresses us. We are responsible—that is, we must make a response. We may choose to say yes and thus fulfill the Creator's glorious purpose for us, or we may say no and violate it. This is what is meant by moral responsibility. God calls us to freedom, fulfillment, and joy—but we can refuse them. In a deep mystery, hidden in God's purposes for man before the foundation of the world, lies the truth of man's free will and God's sovereignty. This much we know: a God who is sovereign chose to create a man capable of willing his own freedom and therefore capable of answering the call.

Jesus, in response to the will of the Father, demonstrated what it means to be fully human when He took upon Himself the form of a man and in so doing voluntarily and gladly chose both dependence and obedience. Humanity for us, as for Christ, means both dependence and obedience.

The unwillingness on the part of men and women to acknowledge their helpless dependence is a violation of our "creatureliness." The unwillingness to be obedient is a violation of our humanity. Both are declarations of independence and, whether physical or moral, are essentially atheistic. In both, the answer to the call is no.

Bishop Frank Houghton's lovely hymn expresses the dependence and obedience of the Son to the Father:

> Thou who wast rich beyond all splendor,
>   All for love's sake becamest poor;
> Thrones for a manger didst surrender,
>   Sapphire-paved courts for stable floor.
>
> Thou who art God beyond all praising,
>   All for love's sake becamest Man;
> Stooping so low, but sinners raising
>   Heavenwards by Thine eternal plan.
>
> Thou who art love beyond all telling,
>   Savior and King, we worship Thee!
> Immanuel, within us dwelling,
>   Make us what Thou wouldst have us be.

Discipline is the wholehearted yes to the call of God. When I know myself called, summoned, addressed, taken possession of, known, acted upon, I have heard the Master. I put myself gladly, fully, and forever at His disposal, and to whatever He says my answer is yes.

THREE

How Do We Know We Are Called?

I AM PULLED or drawn by Christ's call rather as the earth is pulled by the force of gravity. It is helpful to remember that the same word that is used for this mysterious force is also used to mean "seriousness" or "earnestness." It is a force that draws toward a center. As I respond to that force and move in accordance with it, I am no longer weightless. I am serious, earnest, "grave." The same truth applies both to the spiritual and physical worlds. In space, astronauts experience the misery of having no reference point, no force that draws them to the center. The effort of performing ordinary activities without the help of that pull is often vastly greater than it would be under normal conditions (try pouring a glass of water, eating a sunny-side-up egg, or turning a screwdriver—water will not fall, the egg will not stay on your fork, the screwdriver will not revolve: *you* will). Where there is no "moral gravity"—that is, no force that draws us to the center—there is spiritual weightlessness. We float on feelings that will carry us where we never meant to go; we bubble with emotional experiences that we often take for spiritual ones; and we are puffed up with pride. Instead of seriousness, there is foolishness. Instead of gravity, flippancy. Sentimentality takes the place of theology. Our reference point will never serve to keep our feet on solid rock, for our reference point, until we answer God's call, is merely ourselves. We cannot possibly tell which end is up. Paul calls them fools who ". . . measure themselves by themselves, to find in themselves their own standard of comparison!"

How do we know that we are called? This question is asked again and again, the answers given being widely varied and confusing. The New Testament contains many expressions of the Christian's calling:

. . . You who have heard the call and belong to Jesus Christ.

Called . . . to share in the life of . . . Jesus Christ our Lord.

My brothers, think what sort of people you are, whom God has called. . . .

. . . The call to be a Christian. . . .

. . . Called . . . to liberty. . . .

. . . Called to be free men. . . .

. . . Live up to your calling.

. . . To this peace you were called. . . .

Who were these people to whom Paul was writing in each of these phrases? Were they a special breed, marked, perhaps, by notable gifts and physical perfection? We know that they were ordinary people, people who had been, before they believed, all kinds of sinners. How could Paul be so sure that they were "called"? Why, by their obedience, of course. Certainty comes with obedience. It is only through action that the call of God is known. The invitations have been issued:

Come to me, all whose work is hard, whose load is heavy; and I will give you relief. Bend your necks to my yoke, and learn from me, for I am gentle and humble-hearted. . . .

20

... If anyone is thirsty, let him come to me; whoever believes in me, let him drink.

"He called the people to him, as well as his disciples, and said to them, 'Anyone who wishes to be a follower of mine must leave self behind; he must take up his cross, and come with me." It is important to note that this call was issued to both the common people and the disciples. "Anyone who wishes" could come, if he would accept the conditions.

We need never ask the question, "How do I know I'm called?" We ought rather to ask, "How do I know I am *not* called?" We are required to take the risk, move, trust God, make a beginning. This is what Jesus always asked of those who came to Him for help of any kind. Sometimes He asked them to state their case ("What do you want me to do?"), to affirm their desire ("Do you want to be healed?"), and often to *do* something positive ("Stretch out your hand") before He could do His work. There had to be evidence of faith, some kind of beginning on their part. The first baby step of faith is followed by a daily walk of obedience, and it is as we continue with Him in His Word that we are assured that we were, in fact, called and have nothing to fear. The commonest fear of the true disciple, I suppose, is his own unworthiness. When Paul wrote to the Corinthians, a group of Christians who had made some terrible messes even inside the church itself, he still never doubted their calling; for they were prepared to hear the Word and to be guided and corrected. It was not the *perfection* of their faith that convinced him they were called. They had made a beginning. In that beginning, Paul found evidence of faith: "It is in full reliance upon God, through Christ, that we make such claims. There is no question of our being qualified in ourselves: we cannot claim anything as our own. The qualification we have comes from God."

Young people sometimes say to me, "I'll just die if the

Lord calls me to be a missionary," or words to that effect.

"Wonderful!" I say. "That's the best possible way to start. You won't be of much use on the mission field unless you 'die' first." The conditions for discipleship begin with "dying," and if you take the first step, very likely you will find that you have indeed been "called."

Desire and conviction both play a part in vocation. Often the desire comes first. There may be a natural inclination or an interest aroused by information or perhaps an unexplained longing. If these sometimes-deceptive feelings are offered to the Master and subjected to the test of His Word, they will be confirmed by various means and become a conviction. Sometimes the conviction comes first, accompanied not always by desire but by fear or dread, as in the case of Old Testament prophets who were given very hard assignments. The only thing to do then is arise and go.

In C. S. Lewis's *Prince Caspian,* the child Lucy, having gotten lost with her brothers and sister, has at last found the great Lion, shining white in the moonlight. The others had not been able to see him on other occasions, and Lucy was sure they would not believe that she had found him this time.

> "Now, child," said Aslan, ... "I will wait here. Go and wake the others and tell them to follow. If they will not, then you at least must follow me alone."
>
> It is a terrible thing to have to wake four people, all older than yourself and all very tired, for the purpose of telling them something they probably won't believe and making them do something they certainly won't like. "I mustn't think about it, I must just do it," thought Lucy.

She does it, and eventually they follow her. When they find Aslan, he looked "so majestic that they felt as glad as anyone can who feels afraid, and as afraid as anyone can who feels glad."

For Lucy, believing was seeing. The others could not at first because they would not. It is always thus. The believer alone will be able to hear the call. It comes from beyond ourselves, beyond our society, beyond the climate of opinion and prejudice and rebellion and skepticism in which we live, beyond our time and taste. It draws toward the center of all things, that still place of which T. S. Eliot wrote:

> Against the Word the unstilled world still whirled
> About the centre of the silent Word.

FOUR

Under Orders

CHRISTIAN DISCIPLINE means placing oneself under orders. It is no mere business of self-improvement, to be listed along with speed-reading, weight watching, jogging, time management, home repairs, or how to win friends. Such programs have a strong appeal that is largely self-serving: what's in it for me? Will I improve my IQ, my looks, my build, my efficiency, my house, my bank account? Will I be better liked, courted, taken more seriously, promoted? If these are the goals, certainly it helps to pursue them with the encouragement of and in the company of others with the same ambitions. Social pressure goes a long way, but in the end a do-it-yourself program depends on willpower alone, which is not enough for most of us.

The disciple is one who has made a very simple decision. Jesus invites us to follow Him, and the disciple accepts the invitation. I do not say it is an *easy* decision, and I have found that it needs to be renewed daily. The conditions are not such as attract multitudes. Jesus stated them:

1. He must leave self behind
2. he must take up his cross
3. and come with me

The result of the decision is guaranteed:

1. Whoever cares for his own safety is lost
2. but if a man will let himself be lost for my sake, he will find his true self

The disciple is not on his own, left to seek *self-actualization,* which is a new word for old-fashioned *selfishness.* He is not "doing his thing" to find his own life or liberty or happiness. He gives himself to a Master and in so doing leaves self behind. Any ordinary life in any ordinary town provides ample opportunity to do this. Riding on a New York bus recently, I saw a woman reach over and slide open a small section of a window. The bus was very crowded, and I was glad for a little fresh air. The window was angrily slammed shut by another woman.

"It's not really cold out," said the first. "Can't we have a little air?"

"Not on *my* back you can't," came the reply, a perfectly natural one.

The disciple, however, lives by a different rule, a rule not natural to anyone who is a sinner. He will let himself be "lost." It is the great principle of the cross that he takes up— out of his own loss comes another's gain, out of his discomfort another's comfort. How easily we profess a willingness to follow, imagining some notable work for God, some great martyrdom—but forget the first condition the minute there is a little cold air on the back of the neck.

When I was in college, it was the custom when the yearbook came out to ask one's friends to autograph it. Usually they wrote a few words in addition to their signature, and when a girl asked for the autograph of a man she especially admired, she secretly hoped for some clue to his feelings toward her in the words he wrote. Jim Elliot signed his name in my Wheaton *Tower* and added only a Scripture reference: 2 Timothy 2:4.

"A soldier on active service will not let himself be involved in civilian affairs; he must be wholly at his commanding officer's disposal." The message was loud and clear. Any hopes I might have entertained, any feelings Jim himself might have had for me that he had not at that time expressed, must give way before the guiding principle of his life. He was not at liberty to plan the future, being at the disposal of someone else.

Any "soldier," any candidate for Christian discipline, ought daily to report to his commanding officer for duty. At your service, Lord. What the soldier does for the officer is not in the category of a favor. The officer may ask anything. He disposes of the soldier as he chooses. The very thought strikes horror to the modern mind. "Nobody's going to tell *me* what to do. Nobody has a right to dispose of *me.*"

This pattern of thinking has its powerful effect on Christians as well, so that we have come to imagine that discipleship is somehow an "extra." We suppose that we can be Christians, going to church, saying our prayers, singing those sweet songs about loving and feeling and sharing and praising, without taking our share of hardship. Those who wish to make a special bid for sainthood, we tell ourselves, might try discipline ("it has its place") as though it were an odd or fanatical life-style, not the thing for most of us.

It is as though we might be Christian without being disciples.

"Yes, I want to be a Christian, but no, I don't want to be Your disciple, Lord. Not yet, anyway. It's a bit much to expect."

"Yes, I'll be a disciple, but no, I certainly don't want to leave self behind."

"I'll leave self behind if You say so, Lord, but don't ask me to take up any crosses. I'm not sure I'd feel comfortable with that."

26

"Follow You, Lord? Well, yes, sure—but let me have a little input, won't You, about where we're going?"

Nothing could be further from the spirit of the Gospel. The very reason Christ died ". . . was that men, while still in life, should cease to live for themselves, and should live for him who for their sake died and was raised to life."

To be a Christian in New Testament terms is to be a disciple. There are no two ways about it. We have a Savior who has forgiven and saved us from the penalty of sin. Most of us would happily settle for that. But He died to save us also from our *sins,* many of which we love and hate to part with. Christ could not have done this if He were not Lord over all the powers of evil. Jesus Christ is Savior because He is Lord. He is Lord because He is Savior. I cannot be saved from my sins unless I am also saved from myself, so Christ must be "commanding officer" in my life.

Grace, Book, Spirit— And One Thing More

AN OVERWEIGHT WOMAN told me she had prayed for years that God would take away her appetite. He didn't. She continued to gain weight until she was disgusted with herself.

"Lord, why don't You answer my prayer and take away the desire to eat?" she asked.

"Then what would *you* have to do?" He asked her.

"I saw at once that *I* had a responsibility. I wouldn't have had any if I had had no temptation to eat. I realized God was not going to make it that easy for me—I had to start disciplining myself and trust Him to help me with my decision."

God does not make all the moves for us. He provides the means to discipline. Will discipline, then, save us? No, it is Christ who saves us. We need to be very clear about this. From the earliest days of Christianity people have fallen into the error of thinking of discipline as the means to salvation.

Salvation is a gift, purely a gift, forever a gift. It is grace and nothing else that obtains it for us. Discipline is not my claim on Christ, but the evidence of His claim on me. I do not "make" Him Lord, I acknowledge Him Lord. To do this in honesty involves the full intention to do His will, that is, to live under the discipline of His Word. But even that is not something we manage all by ourselves. Three things help us.

If we are Christians, we are under *grace*. We are disciplined by grace. "The grace of God has dawned upon the world . . .

and by it we are *disciplined* to renounce godless ways and worldly desires, and to live a life of temperance, honesty, and godliness. . . ."

If we are Christians we have a rule *book*. We are disciplined by the book. "Every inspired scripture has its use . . . for reformation of manners and *discipline* in right living."

If we are Christians we have the *Spirit* of God. We are disciplined by that Spirit. "The spirit that God gave us is no craven spirit, but one to inspire . . . *self-discipline.*"

There it is. The grace makes it possible; the Scripture points the way; the Spirit inspires—but there is one thing more. Yet still there is something for *man* to do, and it is the greatest thing any man can ever do. It is to put his full trust in the living God. Faith is the only thing required.

There is something that pretends to be Christianity which is mostly a mood. The measure of its faith is merely the measure of its feeling.

"I love the feeling that I get when I get together with God's wonderful people" is a song that describes all some people know about faith. When the feeling is there, they've got it. When the feeling is gone, they've lost it.

James puts it very plainly in his epistle:

My brothers, what use is it for a man to say he has faith when he does nothing to show it? Can that faith save him? Suppose a brother or a sister is in rags with not enough food for the day, and one of you says, "Good luck to you, keep yourselves warm, and have plenty to eat," but does nothing to supply their bodily needs, what is the good of that? So with faith; if it does not lead to action, it is in itself a lifeless thing.

But someone may object: "Here is one who claims to have faith and another who points to his deeds." To which I reply:

"Prove to me that this faith you speak of is real though not accompanied by deeds, and by my deeds I will prove to you my faith." You have faith enough to believe that there is one God. Excellent! The devils have faith like that, and it makes them tremble. But can you not see, you quibbler, that faith divorced from deeds is barren? Was it not by his action, in offering his son Isaac upon the altar, that our father Abraham was justified? Surely you can see that faith was at work in his actions, and that by these actions the integrity of his faith was fully proved.

That faith is neither a mood nor a feeling, but practical obedience is clearly seen when Jesus puts the responsibility of forgiveness squarely before the apostles—seven times in one day, He told them, they must forgive the same man. They recognized dimly that this was going to require faith and theirs did not amount to much. Mood and feeling would not go far toward enabling them to obey that command. "Lord, increase our faith!" they said, very likely taking refuge from obedience by implying that they could not possibly be expected to obey until, by some special miracle of grace, they were given a superabundance of faith. Superabundance indeed! Why, even faith no bigger than a mustard seed could uproot a mulberry tree, Jesus told them. The way to increase their faith was to get busy and do what they were supposed to do, and ". . . when you have carried out all your orders, you should say, 'We are servants and deserve no credit; we have only done our duty.' "

There is not much of that spirit around today. We do not recognize mastery. We do not see ourselves as at the disposal of the Lord. We expect appreciation. We would like at least a thank-you, and perhaps an approving little pat.

". . . If I were trying to win human approval," Paul wrote,

"I should never be Christ's servant." It is to the One who is in charge that we owe an account of what we do, not to spectators. When a servant renders service, it is merely what is expected. There is nothing out of the ordinary about it.

A couple I know had been married only a week or two when the wife went out shopping. The husband wondered what he might do for her while she was gone that would please and surprise her and show her how much he loved her. A brilliant plan came to mind. He got down on hands and knees and scrubbed the kitchen floor. It was a demeaning task in his opinion, and he felt exceedingly humble while performing it. How amazed Ann would be! He waited in eager anticipation of her return, thinking how blessed it is to give.

She drove in the driveway, breezed into the kitchen, set the grocery bags on the counter, and glanced at the floor.

"Oh—the floor's clean. Thank you, honey!" was all she said and went about putting things away.

The man told me he went into a three-day funk. He was hurt; he was insulted; he was not properly appreciated; and the blessing of giving drained out in an instant because he had not received the kind of thanks he had expected.

Ann had no idea what the trouble was. What *she* did not know was that her husband had never heard of a man's doing such a thing as scrubbing a floor for his wife, especially voluntarily, having thought of it all by himself. What *he* did not know was that in his wife's family, no woman ever did the job. Her father considered it a man's job and did it as a matter of course.

That young husband took the lesson to heart. He now believes that it would be wise for every Christian to post as his motto the lesson Jesus taught: "We are servants and deserve no credit; we have only done our duty."

We have been given a task. Faith is that task. Let us not deceive ourselves into thinking we are making any contribution to our eternal salvation, are doing God a favor, or that He owes us anything for work done.

> It is by His grace you are saved, through trusting him; it is not your own doing. It is God's gift, not a reward for work done. There is nothing for anyone to boast of. For we are God's handiwork, created in Christ Jesus to devote ourselves to the good deeds for which God has designed us.

Designed for good deeds. It's as simple as that. It was God's idea. He did the designing. He expects us to work, just as the designer of a precision instrument, if he understands the principles involved and designs it accordingly, expects the thing to work. It is no great credit to the instrument if it does.

SIX

A Sovereign God and a Man's Choice

THE ANALOGY of the instrument breaks down. It may help us to understand the will of the Creator and His absolute power over what He makes, but it leaves out the will of man. It would not be possible, within the scope of this book, to deal adequately or well with the question of God's sovereignty, even if I were equipped to do so. I am not so equipped. But perhaps I can point out some things that have helped me to grasp certain aspects of this theological mystery.

If God is in control of the big things, He must also be in control of the little ones. It is nonsense to say that He controls winds, storms, and oceans, but not the pressures that move them, or that He sets the boundaries of the sea and causes the tides to swell and sink, but has nothing to do with individual waves, with the creatures that swim in them or with the intricacies of molecules and atoms that make up the whole.

Recently I learned about a wondrous small creature called a diatom. It is a one-celled speck of algae, the largest diatom being only one millimeter in diameter. They have been called the most vital "plants" on earth, though since they swim and dig, there is room for debate as to whether this is an accurate label. They provide more food than any other living thing, but if all the Designer had in mind was fodder, he need not have made them so fancy. Diatoms come in a tremendous variety of shapes, including pinwheels, spirals, disks, rods, ovals, triangles, and even stars and chandeliers. Many tiny creatures eat them, including copepods and krills (which I had never heard of until I learned about diatoms). Fish eat them, and so do humpback whales, which manage to swill down several hundred billion diatoms every few hours. Killer whales love them, but it takes five tons of the little stars and chandeliers and things to make one pound of killer whale.

Who constructed this astonishing food chain?

Albert Einstein wrote, "A spirit is manifest in the laws of the universe, vastly superior to that of man, and one in the face of which we with our modest powers must feel humble. Causality has to exist. The universe could not operate on chance. God does not play dice."

God, the causer of it all, also "causes us to cause."

"The self-determining power of the individual is part of the ordered predestination of God and of the necessity *felt by His love* to endow man with a freedom like His own if He expected man to respond to His own."

The story is told of a preacher who went out to see a wheat farm. As he and the farmer stood looking over the beautiful waves of grain the preacher said, "Well, John, you and God have surely done a good job here."

The farmer pushed his hat back on his head, gazed silently at the field, and said slowly, "You shoulda seen it when God had it by Himself."

Next to the Incarnation, I know of no more staggering and humbling truth than that a sovereign God has ordained my participation. This is the order of the universe: every creature given its rightful place, each contributing its part to the whole, man among them. Yet man is unique in having been charged with tremendous liberty. The farmer made up his own mind to plant wheat. The field would not have been there if he had not made the decision and done the prodigious amount of work necessary to produce that shimmering crop. Neither would it have been there if God had not provided the earth in the first place, commanded sun to shine and rain to fall, and quickened the life of the seed John put in the soil.

We have said that Christian discipline is one's wholehearted yes to the call of God. It is of the highest importance that we understand the necessity of *two* wills, the one created by the other and ordained free, both operating in accord. If we forget that there are two and dwell only on the sovereign will of God, we will abdicate our responsibility and lapse into the fatalism of Islam, which leaves all to the inscrutable and unknowable. If, on the other hand, we forget the sovereignty of God and see ourselves as independent, we will arrogate to ourselves all responsibility and leave God out of it—in other words, we make ourselves God. In both cases we fail to do His will, and the result is the forfeiting of our joy and freedom.

God has arranged things in such a way that His own action is coupled with the action of men. The Bible is replete with examples of a loving and powerful God choosing sinful and weak men to accomplish His purposes, allowing them the dignity to act in freedom and thus to have a *willed* part in what He does.

When the people of Israel found themselves "between the devil and the deep blue sea," that is, between the Egyptians and the Red Sea, they were in despair. They were furious at Moses for getting them into this mess. Moses promised that the Lord would save them if they would only be still. He was correct. The Lord did save them, but not without cooperation, that is, acts of obedience on the part of both Moses and the people.

"Tell the people to go forward," God said. Moses had to believe God meant it, and he had to do what God said. If he had doubted, all would have been lost. Moses trusted God, and the people trusted Moses. They also had to obey.

"Lift up your rod and stretch out your hand over the sea and divide it," God said. Moses surely must have been thinking, My *rod?* My *hand? What can possibly be the use of either in a situation like this?* He stood between an irresistible force and an immovable object, and how rod or hand could stop the one or budge the other he could not imagine. But he obeyed. The sovereignty of God came into action. A wind arose and did God's bidding. The sea also obeyed, and the Egyptians were drowned and the Israelites saved. Here is sovereign power—over one man, over a people, over the elements of nature, over an enemy. But here, too, is a man acting in freedom.

"I have determined to make an end of all flesh. . . ," God said to a man named Noah, who walked with Him. "Make yourself an ark. . . . I will establish my covenant with you. . . ." Noah did it. His willingness to act in accordance with God's instructions meant the salvation of the human race and of all species of animal. Noah's willed action and his faith went hand in hand. We see again that faith is a far cry from feeling or religious mood. It is not vague. It hears the Word of the Lord, and it acts. ". . . If it does not lead to action, it is in itself a lifeless thing."

We say that *Noah* built the ark, *Noah* saved his family and all the animals. From a spiritual standpoint, it was faith that built the ark, faith that saved the family, faith that put the whole world in the wrong, and faith that put Noah into Hebrews 11, that gallery of portraits showing what faith looks like. Noah knew his sovereign.

When the will of man acts in accord with the will of God, that is faith. When the will of man acts in opposition to the will of God, that is unbelief.

God could have chosen to do everything Himself, but instead He so conceived the world that birds must build nests and sit on eggs, microbes must break down organisms, salmon must struggle upstream to spawn, earthworms must aerate the soil, bees must construct honeycombs, and man must will and work.

It is the willingness we must emphasize here. We pray "Thy will be done on earth *as it is in heaven.*" God's will is always *willingly* and *gladly* done in heaven. Willing obedience is a very different thing from coercion. A college dean once observed that the happiest students on any campus are the musicians and athletes. "Why?" I asked. "Because they're disciplined, and they volunteered to be disciplined." People sitting in required lectures are under discipline, and people sitting in the television lounge are "volunteers," but athletes and musicians put themselves under a coach or director who tells them what to do. They delight to do his will. They are actually having fun.

God does not coerce us to follow Him. He invites us. He wills that we should will—that is, He *wills our freedom* to decline or to accept. If we want to be disciples, we place ourselves, like the football player and the instrumentalist, under someone's direction. He tells us what to do, and we find our happiness in doing it. We will not find it anywhere else. We will not find it by doing only what we want to do and not doing what we don't want to do. That is the popular idea of what freedom is, but it does not work. Freedom lies in keeping the rules. Joy is there, too. (If only we could keep the joy in view!) The violinist in the orchestra has submitted first to the instructor. He obeys the rules laid down by him and handles his instrument accordingly. He submits then to the music as written by the composer, paying attention to the markings for dynamics as well as to notes, rests, and timing.

Finally, he submits to the conductor. The conductor tells him, by word or gesture, what he wants, and the violinist does just that.

Is there any image of freedom and joy more exhilarating than a full orchestra, everybody sawing, tootling, pounding, strumming, blowing, clashing, and hammering away for all they are worth, under the direction of the immense energy and discipline of a man who knows every note of every instrument in every concerto and knows how to elicit that note exactly so that it will contribute most fully to the glory of the work as a whole? Compare that image, for example, with other pursuits of "happiness": a county fair on a hot Sunday afternoon, America at leisure, standing in line for cotton candy, standing in line for the roller coaster, standing in line for tickets to the Blue Grass concert, shuffling and elbowing through the sweating mobs, babies in strollers crying for ice cream, toddlers screaming for more rides, exhausted parents, vacant-looking teenagers, bored senior citizens, everybody harried by the teeming crowd, deafened by the noise (hawkers, shooting galleries, fun machines, amplified music played at the highest possible decible), looking for fun. Everybody is "free," so to speak, to do his own thing, and the result is chaos and cacophony. The first image, I must confess— where nobody is doing his own thing but everybody is free *because* he obeys—is somehow vastly more appealing to me.

It is a great relief when somebody else is in charge. He knows what he's doing, and all you need to do is follow directions. You do not rebel at his telling you what to do. You are glad to be told. He knows more than you do, knows the best way to accomplish what you want to accomplish, and you are sure you will be better off with him than without him, happier by obeying than by disobeying.

Because we had accepted an invitation from the bishop of Norwich, we were allowed to go, guided by a young verger, up into Norwich Cathedral's tower where the public was not admitted. It helps to know somebody in charge. We gladly submitted to his direction.

We did not climb the tower expecting to be shut up in a dungeon, kept on bread and water, and finally axed to death. Both Lars and I wanted to see the view of the cathedral close, the town, and the lovely Norfolk countryside. There was another pleasure I was seeking—that of entering secret places, sensing the mystery of hidden staircases. Neither of us was disappointed.

God will never disappoint us. He loves us and has only one purpose for us: holiness, which in His kingdom equals joy. Had Lars and I harbored any suspicion that the bishop meant to do us harm or that the verger did not know where he was going, we would certainly not have followed him into the dark passageways. If deep in our hearts we suspect that God does not love us and cannot manage our affairs as well as we can, we certainly will not submit to His discipline.

We know that He loves us. Jesus Christ, nailed to a cross, is irrefutable proof of that. Let us never think He was "martyred" to appease an angry God, for "... God was in Christ reconciling the world to himself...."

The view from the tower would be a poor comparison with what God offers us. It is on the basis of a solid conviction that He is both sovereign and loving that we commit ourselves to Him unconditionally, believing that what we leave behind is less than nothing compared to what we hope for. Paul declared that everything he had ever gained was "useless rubbish" compared to learning to know Christ. The man who buys a field and finds in it a treasure sells without a qualm everything he possesses in order to purchase the field. This is what the Kingdom of God is like. The view from the tower was well worth the climb.

But let us think about the climb itself.

39

There are those who do not want to receive Christ. Those who do, however, are given not an "instant kingdom," but the "... right to *become* children of God...." Here is the truth of divine sovereignty and human responsibility wrapped up in a single verse. To those who *will* He gives. There are many levels of meaning here that we cannot explore. It does not say God makes them instant children of God. It says He gives them the right to become. To those who receive Him, to those who have yielded to Him their allegiance, He gives the right to *become* children of God. Peter wrote, "... You, because you put your faith in God, are under the protection of his power until salvation comes...." The writer to the Hebrews refers to certain ones in whom the good news "... did no good, because it met with no faith in those who heard it." These references show how foolish it is to suppose that you can be a Christian without the trouble of discipleship or that you can "get to heaven" without bothering to be obedient. Is my obedience, then, what opens heaven's door to me? No. Is it my will, after all, that determines my salvation? No. The children of God are born, "... not of blood, nor of the will of the flesh nor of the will of man, but of God." "It does not depend on man's will or effort, but on God's mercy."

If we hold back our obedience until we have plumbed the theological depths of this mystery, we shall be disobedient. There are truths that cannot be known except by doing them. The Gospels show many cases of those who wished to understand rather than to obey. Jesus had scathing words for them. On one occasion He turned from them to those who had already believed in Him and said, "If you dwell within the revelation I have brought, *you* are indeed my disciples; *you* shall know the truth, and the truth will set *you* free."

To "dwell within the revelation" surely means living by what we have been shown. It means hearing and doing.

Another aspect of the climb is suffering.

To the unbeliever, the fact of suffering only convinces him that God is not to be trusted, does not love us. To the believer, the opposite is true. "I know, O Lord, that thy judgments are right, and that in faithfulness thou hast afflicted me," the psalmist cried.

One reference to the Thessalonian Christians' persecution shows clearly how even injustice on the human level serves the justice of God in bringing His servants to holiness. The believers in Thessalonica had responded to trouble with a steadfast faith and an increased love. "See how this brings out the justice of God's judgement," writes Paul. "It will prove you worthy of the kingdom of God, for which indeed you are suffering." He goes on to assure them that the account would some day be balanced. There would be punishment for those who refused to acknowledge God, and glory for believers. Paul prayed for them, ". . . that our God may count you worthy of his calling, and mightily bring to fulfillment every good purpose and every act inspired by faith."

We see here the clear fact of a sovereign will, operating sometimes through and sometimes in spite of believers and unbelievers, both in the present and in the future. What the persecutors were doing to the believers was evil. Yet for Christ's sake the believers endured it and were thus proving themselves "worthy of the kingdom of God." He had not let go of them. Nothing could separate them from His love. His sovereignty held them fast. They, for their part, willed to endure, holding themselves expendable for the sake of Him who expended Himself for them. Finally, the prayers of Paul also were an essential element in the full working out of God's purpose, God having set up the world in such a way that prayer is *necessary* even to His own plans.

A few of the many verses in which we see the harmony of the two wills at work are these:

Gideon said to God, "If *thou* wilt deliver Israel through *me* as thou hast promised."

So we prayed to our God, *and* posted a guard day and night against them.

I also put all *my energy* into the work on this wall. . . . this work had been accomplished by the *help* of our *God.*

Humble *yourselves* then under God's mighty hand, and *he* will lift you up in due time.

These passages speak only of the will in harmony with God, but we cannot ignore God's sovereignty also over the will opposed to Him.

So the king would not listen to the people; for the Lord had given this turn to the affair, in order that the word he had spoken by Ahijah of Shiloh to Jeroboam son of Nebat might be fulfilled.

Herod and Pontius Pilate conspired with the Gentiles and peoples of Israel to do all the things which, under thy hand by thy decree, were foreordained.

You meant to do me harm; but God meant to bring good out of it. . . .

Perhaps the most imponderable words of all are those terrible ones that show the Sovereign Lord at the mercy of men:

The Son of Man is going the way appointed for him in the scriptures, but alas for that man by whom the Son of Man is betrayed! It would be better for that man if he had never been born.

> When he [Jesus] had been given up to you, by the deliber-
> ate will and plan of God, you used heathen men to crucify
> and kill him.

The Bible does not explain everything necessary for our intellectual satisfaction, but it explains everything necessary for our obedience and hence for God's satisfaction.

A young woman asked the great preacher Charles Spurgeon if it was possible to reconcile God's sovereignty and man's responsibility. "Young woman," said he. "You don't reconcile friends."

SEVEN

The Discipline of the Body

A TELEVISION COMMERCIAL shows a man springing out of bed, racing down the stairs, gulping a cup of coffee, snatching up coat and briefcase, and exploding out the front door. The message: "The day can't begin soon enough for a man compelled by a single aim in life." He's a Bache broker. He can't wait to get to the office to find out what's happening on the market, but grabs the kitchen phone and asks, "How did we open in London today?"

The lust for money and power moves men when a bulldozer wouldn't move them otherwise. They will punish their bodies, spending most of their waking hours sitting in an office chair, then working out furiously in a gymnasium or on a jogging track, eating tiny breakfasts, tremendous "business" lunches, and high-calorie dinners, all in order to get ahead in the world and enjoy some of its pleasures for a season.

Holiness has never been the driving force of the majority. It is, however, mandatory for anyone who wants to enter the Kingdom. "Aim at . . . a holy life, for without that no one will see the Lord."

"For you know what orders we gave you, in the name of the Lord Jesus," wrote Paul to the Thessalonians. "This is the will of God, that you should be holy: you must abstain from fornication; each one of you must learn to gain mastery over his body, to hallow and honour it, not giving way to lust

44

like the pagans who are ignorant of God. . . . For God called us to holiness, not to impurity."

Discipline, for a Christian, begins with the body. We have only one. It is this body that is the primary material given to us for sacrifice. If we didn't have this, we wouldn't have anything. We are meant to present it, offer it up, give it unconditionally to God for His purposes. This, we are told, is an "act of spiritual worship." The giving of this physical body, comprising blood, bone, and tissue, worth a few dollars in chemicals, becomes a spiritual act, "for such is the worship which you, as rational creatures, should offer."

The Jerusalem Bible translates it this way: "Think of God's mercy, my brothers, and worship Him, I beg you, in a way that is worthy of thinking beings," [that is, a note tells us, " 'in a spiritual way,' as opposed to the ritual sacrifices of Jews or pagans"] "by offering your living bodies as a holy sacrifice. . . ."

More spiritual failure is due, I believe, to this cause than to any other: the failure to recognize this living body as having anything to do with worship or holy sacrifice. This body is, quite simply, the starting place. Failure here is failure everywhere else.

"He who would see the face of the most powerful Wrestler, our boundless God," wrote Arozco, "must first have wrestled with himself."

Only one who has taken seriously the correlation between the physical and spiritual and begun the struggle can appreciate the aptness of that word *wrestle*. Habits, for example, hold a half nelson on us. That hold must be broken if we are to be free for the Lord's service. We cannot give our hearts to God and keep our bodies for ourselves.

What sort of body is this?

It's mortal. It will not last. It was made of dust to begin

with and after death will return to dust. Paul called it a "vile" body, or one "belonging to our humble state," a "body of sin," a "dead" body because of sin. But it is also a temple or shrine for the Holy Spirit; it is a "member" of Christ's body. It is, furthermore—and this makes all the difference in how we should treat it—wholly redeemable, transfigurable, "resurrectible."

The Christian's body houses not only the Holy Spirit Himself, but the Christian's heart, will, mind, and emotions—all that plays a part in our knowing God and living for Him.

In my case, the "house" is tall; it is Anglo-Saxon, middle-aged, and female. I was not asked about my preferences in any of these factors, but I was given a choice about the use I make of them. In other words, the body was a gift to me. Whether I will thank God for it and offer it as a holy sacrifice is for me to decide.

What is meant by disciplining the body?

A body needs food. Food is a question of discipline for us who live in very rich, very civilized, very self-indulgent countries. For those who have not the vast array of choices we have, food is a fundamental matter of subsistence and not a major hindrance to holiness.

Discipline is evident on every page of the life of Daniel. The story starts with his being chosen as one of a group of young men from noble and royal families in Israel to serve in the palace of Nebuchadnezzar, king of Babylon. The first thing that sets Daniel apart from the others is his decision not to eat the rich food provided for them by the royal household, but only vegetables and water. He did not want to be defiled. It must have been God who put the idea into Daniel's head. It was certainly God who made the master show kindness and goodwill toward Daniel by granting his request. It was the beginning of the Lord's preparation of a man whose spiritual fiber would be rigorously tested later on.

It is significant that only 10 percent of our nation's top executives are overweight. This seems to me to indicate that few men who have not succeeded in curbing the appetite will make it to the top. Physical restraint is basic to power. They do it for power in this world. We do it for power in another.

Christians ought to watch what they eat. I do not refer here only to overeating, which is a bad thing, but to eating the wrong things. Too many sweets, too many rich things, too much junk. Take a walk through any supermarket and note the space given to soft drinks, candy, packaged snack foods, dry cereals. We could do very well without any of these. Try it for a week. You may be surprised at how dependent you are on them. You might even discover that you are an addict.

As a missionary I lived most of the time in fairly remote regions of the South American jungle, where the food that was available was all "natural." We ate a lot of manioc, a starchy tuber cultivated by the Indians, which provided their "staff of life." We ate rice, beans, pineapples, papayas, eggs, and whatever meat might be available from time to time, which was not often. There were no prepared foods to fall back on. No between-meal snacks. We had sugar, brought in from the outside, which we used to make lemonade wherever lemons were grown. We also imported oatmeal, powdered milk, salt, flour, and sometimes luxuries like cheese and chocolate. But menus were relatively simple, and our health was always excellent. It is a good thing, it seems to me, to learn to do with less.

One way to begin to see how vastly indulgent we usually are is to fast.

Fasting was prescribed by Jewish law and has always been a part of Christian practice.

A friend of mine recounted how she had been hammering away at heaven's door for the answer to a certain prayer. Nothing seemed to be happening. She began to get angry at God because He wasn't doing anything. Then He seemed to say quietly, "Why don't you fast?"

"Then it came over me," she said. "I didn't really *care* that much."

Another friend said she disagreed thoroughly with the notion of fasting, because it was nothing more than an attempt to "twist God's arm." "He knows what I need, and if He wants to give it to me, He can. There's no need to become an ascetic."

There is little understanding today of the real purpose of hermits and anchorites. While there were undoubtedly some who thought to buy their way to heaven by crucifying the flesh, the true effectiveness was based on their willingness to serve by giving themselves wholly to prayer and contemplation. This involves sacrifice of one kind or another, today as yesterday. Hermits and anchorites chose solitude, poverty, withdrawal from the world, fasting. In some of the churches of England there still exist anchorages—cells in which anchorites were walled up for life. One such can still be seen at Chester-le-Street Parish Church, in the north of England. Food was passed to him; sometimes people spoke to him through an aperture; and he had a "squint," a slit in the wall through which he could observe mass in the church. The people of the town rejoiced to know that someone was always at prayer.

I know Christians who fast on a regular basis—one day a week, one meal a week, one meal a month, or on certain days of the church calendar. I know others who have found it very helpful to fast when they have some special matter for prayer—a difficult decision to make, a new project to begin, a sick friend they want to help.

In Antioch God told the disciples, while they were fasting, to set apart Barnabas and Saul. Then, "... after further fasting and prayer ... ," they laid their hands on them and sent them off to do the work to which God had specially called them. In Lystra, Iconium, and Antioch, Paul appointed elders and then "... with prayer and fasting committed them to the Lord in whom they had put their faith."

Bishop John Allen has given five good reasons to fast:

1. it helps us to identify with the hungry, whom we are commanded to serve
2. it reminds us to pray
3. it makes us open to God's call
4. it prompts us to reflect on the outworking of His call
5. it is a mysterious instrument of the Holy Spirit's work

There are some things fasting does not do. It has never helped me to forget about eating. In fact, I find myself thinking a great deal about it. (Perhaps I do not fast long enough.) It is a long day that is not broken by the usual three meals. One finds out what an astonishing amount of time is spent in the planning, purchasing, preparing, eating, and cleaning up of meals. The social aspect of fasting is perhaps the most awkward thing about it. Jesus told us not to let people know we are fasting, but to groom ourselves as usual so that only our Father, "... who is in the secret place ..." will see. Sometimes it is quite impossible to keep one's fast a secret. I know one mother of a large family who fasts one day a week, but continues to cook for her family and sits down with them at the table to have a cup of clear tea. Her family is used to this, and does not mind. Some families might. God knows the individual's circumstances and the purpose of heart. In Daniel's case God made it possible for him to carry out his desire.

Fasting will not necessarily enable you to concentrate. It is important not to become agitated with yourself if your mind wanders. Ask the Lord to help you to concentrate on prayer, Bible reading, meditation. When feelings of spiritual pride are detected, confess them. When the phone rings, answer it if you must. When thoughts of next week's meeting intrude, mention them also to God and leave them with Him while you go back to the business of your prayers. Don't be shocked at your own inability to "be spiritual." The greatest saints knew their sinfulness and their weaknesses.

> They who fain would serve Him best
> Are conscious most of wrong within.

Don't try to sit or kneel in one position for too long. Stand up to pray, walk around, go outdoors and pray as you walk. If it is not possible to pray aloud without attracting attention, pray in a whisper. That will be better for most of us than trying to pray only mentally, a method that often encourages little more than wool-gathering.

In ancient Jewish times a stubborn son who was a glutton and a drunkard was stoned to death.

Gluttony, one of the more obvious modern sins, is generally tacitly accepted. Little is said about it from the pulpit. It is too embarrassing; it gets down too close to where the people, often including the preacher, live. No one who is fat dares to preach about it—he has no room to talk. Seldom will one who is not fat have the courage to broach the subject, for he will be told he has no business to talk since he has never "had a weight problem." (How does anyone know? Maybe he practices what he preaches.) Who then is left to talk?

While a very small percentage of people are overweight for physiological reasons, the vast majority simply eat too much of the wrong things. That's the long and the short of it. Calories that are not burned up are stored in fat.

Jean Nidetch, who founded Weight Watchers, said that she did not start solving her problem until she was willing to name it: FAT. She posted little signs all over the house—on mirrors, on the refrigerator, over the sink—FAT, FAT, FAT.

I once wrote an article about a boat trip in which I described one of my fellow passengers as a fat lady. It seems I touched a very sensitive nerve. Seldom do I hear from readers, but I am still getting angry letters about that article. All are from females, several of whom have been careful to explain that they themselves are not fat. "But," wrote one, "I have some chunky friends." I wondered if the friends would appreciate being called "chunky." The Bible says Eglon was a very fat man. Isn't it all right to write about a fat lady? If we see ourselves in her and are offended, it's time to do something about it.

Many a Christian has found the hardly hoped-for strength of the Lord when bringing to Him some very real, very difficult physical need. If weight has quite literally become a "burden," why should we not bring it to the Lord and ask for His help in overcoming it? Can my will not cooperate with His in this matter as in spiritual matters? For some, fasting might be the place where discipline begins, even if they are not overweight. For others, dieting will be the place, whether it means eliminating junk foods for the sake of sounder health or eliminating calories for the sake of a normal weight.

"You do not belong to yourselves. You were bought at a price. Then honour God in your body."

Sleep is another necessity. It takes discipline to go to bed when you ought to, and it takes discipline to get up. Think about your habits. Be honest to God about them, and if you know they are not in line with a disciplined life, pray for His help and start doing something.

My father had a ready answer for those who expressed incredulity at his "ability" to get up so early in the morning: "You have to start the night before."

My great Bible teacher, L. E. Maxwell, was asked by a friend how in the world he had ever "gotten victory" that enabled him to rise at four or five. "How long did it take? Did you have someone pray with you about it?"

"No, I get up," was his reply.

We make a huge joke about our self-indulgence and treat with amusement our failure to pull ourselves out of bed early enough to get to work without a hectic rush. An eighteenth-century hymn by Thomas Ken would seem quaint nowadays:

> Awake my soul, and with the sun
> Thy daily stage of duty run:
> Shake off dull sloth and joyful rise
> To pay thy morning sacrifice.

Most of us do not very easily shake off dull sloth. *"Joyful* rise"? Not very realistic, is it? It does not come naturally for us. But it never did for anybody. We forget that. Dull sloth is natural. Human beings haven't changed much in the whole of human history. So instead of dismissing the hymn writer as hopelessly outdated, might we not ask God for His help in being joyful makers of sacrifice?

"I am my body's sternest master . . . ," Paul said. He put this in the context of athletic contests for which the prize is a crown of fading leaves, but reminded the Corinthians that they were in a different kind of competition—for an eternal crown that cannot fade.

The body needs exercise. "The training of the body does bring limited benefits. . . ."

Pope John Paul praised athletics as a lesson in dealing with life:

> Every type of sport carries within itself a rich patrimony of values, which must be always kept present in order to be realized.
>
> The training in reflection, the proper commitment of one's own energies, the education of will, the control of sensitivity, the methodical preparation, perseverance, resistance, the endurance of fatigue and wounds, the domination of one's own faculties, the sense of joy, acceptance of rules, the spirit of renunciation and solidarity, loyalty to commitment, generosity toward the winners, serenity in defeat, patience towards all—these are a complex of moral realities which demand a true asceticism and validly contribute to forming the human being and the Christian.

In spite of the enormous popularity of organized and professional games, as well as of tennis and golf, I suppose that the overwhelming majority of people over twenty-one do not play anything, at least regularly.

Jogging and other forms of violent individual exercise may be suitable for some. For others they would be extreme. The important thing is to move around somehow. Don't ride when you can walk, and walk briskly. When you can climb stairs instead of taking an elevator, climb them. When you do housework, move quickly. If your life's work requires sitting at a desk most of the day, you will have to arrange to get your body into motion. One very neat device for people who find it hard to get outdoor exercise is a small trampoline, about four feet in diameter, which is low enough to fit under a bed when not in use and on which you can "jog" without the risk of shinsplints or injuries to the joints. A doctor friend gave us one of these as a wedding gift—hoping, I suspect, that if Lars exercised, he might last longer than my other husbands.

The bodies we are given are sexual bodies, equipped for sexual intercourse. Modern advertising never lets us forget this. Popular songs refer to very little else. The fashion business thrives on sexual provocation through dress. But being sexually equipped is not a license for us to use the equipment in any way we choose. Like every other good gift that comes down from the Father of Lights, the gift of sexual activity is meant to be used as He intended, within the clearly defined limits of His purpose, which is marriage. If marriage is not included in God's will for an individual, then sexual activity is not included either.

"What am I supposed to do, then, with all this? I've got so much to give—what if nobody takes it?"

Give it to God.

"But you cannot say that our physical body was made for sexual promiscuity; it was made for God, and God is the Answer to our deepest longings," Paul wrote.

To offer my body to the Lord as a living sacrifice includes offering to Him my sexuality and all that that entails, even my unfulfilled longings.

Today this advice will be laughed out of court by most. Sexual control is regarded as a hang-up from which the truly mature have been liberated. There are those still, however—as there have been in every age—who hold as holy the intimate relationship between a man and a woman, recognizing in it a type of Christ's love for His own bride, His church. As such it is not to be profaned.

This attitude can be held only by the mind's being captive to Christ. It is a miracle of grace. Let us not imagine it is anything less.

Malcolm Muggeridge notes in his diary that Tolstoy "tried to achieve virtue, and particularly continence, through the exercise of his will; St. Augustine saw that, for Man, there is no virtue without a miracle. Thus St. Augustine's asceticism brought him serenity, and Tolstoy's anguish, conflict, and the final collapse of his life into tragic buffoonery."

This body, remember, is to be resurrected. As John Donne pointed out long ago, the immortality of the soul is acceptable to man's natural reason, but the resurrection of the body must be a matter of faith.

Where are all the atoms of the flesh which corrosion or consumption has eaten away? In what furrow or bowel of the earth lie all the ashes of a body burned a thousand years since? In what corner of the sea lies all the jelly of a body drowned in the general flood? What coherence, what sympathy, what dependence maintain any relation or correspondence between that arm that was lost in Europe and that leg that was lost in Africa or Asia with scores of years between?

One humor of our dead body produces worms and those worms exhaust all other humor and then all dies and dries and molders into dust, and that dust is blown into the river and that water tumbles into the sea, which ebbs and flows in infinite revolutions.

Still, God knows in what cabinet every seed pearl lies and in what part of the world every grain of every man's dust lies, and (as His prophet speaks in another case) He beckons for the bodies of His saints, and in the twinkling of an eye that body that was scattered over all the elements has sat down at the right of God in a glorious resurrection.

The knowledge that his body will one day be ". . . sown as an animal body, . . . raised as a spiritual body" ought to give a disciple pause, ought to spur him to think of the use he makes of it in this world. Even though flesh and blood can never possess the Kingdom, think of its particles being "beckoned" to sit down with the Lord some day.

EIGHT

The Discipline of the Mind

IN HER BIOGRAPHY of the seventeenth-century French arch-
bishop François de Fénelon, Katharine Day Little writes,
"Simple and orderly living was the secret of his power and
efficiency, for his austerity was in reality a purposeful and rational expenditure rather than a self-conscious mortification.
It represented the beauty of an orderly and clean mind that
naturally turned away from gaudy gewgaws and the disorder of the unnecessary."

A simple and orderly life represents a clean and orderly
mind. Muddled thinking inevitably results in muddled living. A house that is cluttered is usually lived in by people
whose minds are also cluttered, who need to simplify their
lives. This begins with simplifying and clarifying their
thinking. Mind and life need to be freed from the "disorder
of the unnecessary."

"... Be mentally stripped for action, perfectly self-controlled ...," is what Peter says we must do.

Jesus said that the greatest commandment is "Love the
Lord your God with all your heart, with all your soul, with
all your *mind.*"

We have been discussing making an offering of the body,
which is an act of worship "... offered by *mind* and heart."
The next thing we are to do is to let our minds be "remade"
and our whole nature "transformed." We cannot do this by
ourselves. It is the Holy Spirit who must do the work. But we

must open our minds to that work, submit to His control, think on the things that matter rather than on the things that come to nothing in the end. Here again we see both the necessity of a sovereign God working in and through us and the responsibility of the disciple himself to adapt to what God wants to do.

"There is no expedient to which a man will not resort to avoid the real labor of thinking," wrote Sir Joshua Reynolds. Try following a single idea through to its conclusion. How many detours did you make? How many times did you stop to pass the time of day with another idea, utterly unrelated to the first? How often did you sink into the grass as it were, at the side of the road, and let your mind float with the clouds?

Today as I write I have a perfect environment for thinking. I am in a Norwegian *hytte* (hut) on an inland waterway of Norway's Sørland. There is no human being nearby so far as I know, and if there were, I could not say much more to him than *jeg snakker ikke Norsk* (I don't speak Norwegian). There is no telephone, no mail service, nor any plumbing or electricity. It is almost like being back again in the jungle. Who could ask for a situation more conducive to writing and thinking?

Yet I find my mind wandering to a thousand things that have nothing whatever to do with this chapter. Wondering if it is going to clear up, I go over to check the barometer. I go down to the dock to see if the mink who lives in the bank will show himself again. I pick a few wild flowers to put in a vase—Lars will be here later today (he has been spending some of his time in his home town nearby, Kristiansand). I read a bit of Malcolm Muggeridge's diaries. I fix a peanut-butter sandwich and a very expensive California carrot for lunch. I hear children's voices and go out to listen more closely. (It is wonderful to hear children speak a language foreign to me!)

Before I had even finished that paragraph, I heard a familiar whistle. Lars. He was not supposed to be here for another three hours, but it is a welcome diversion from the thinking I intended to do but always find the hardest part of writing. We drink tea and read mail from Massachusetts, England, Illinois, and Idaho. Now Lars is sharpening the scythe before cutting the grass. Back to the typewriter and thinking.

"... Think your way to a sober estimate based on the measure of faith that God has dealt to each of you." *Think your way to.* Do we know how to *think* our way to anything?

We were traveling in a car with friends, discussing our great friend whom none of us had ever met, C. S. Lewis.

"Lewis *thought*," said the man. "It is amazing what you can come up with by really thinking!"

We agreed. (Who could disagree with that?) There was a long pause. Then his wife said, "You know, I believe that's what's wrong with me. I never *think*. Not really."

Most of us have neither the mental capacity nor the education Lewis had, but we could have the mental discipline "if we had a mind to."

"The failure to cultivate the power of peaceful concentration is the greatest single cause of mental breakdown," the great physician William Osler told the students of Yale one Sunday evening nearly seventy years ago. He urged them to gain power over the mental mechanism by a few hours a day of quiet concentration in routine, in order, and in system. "Concentration is an art of slow acquisition, but little by little the mind is accustomed to habits of slow eating and careful digestion, by which alone you escape the 'mental dyspepsy.'"

Take the words quoted above from Romans for a beginning exercise in thinking. "... Think your way to a sober estimate based on the measure of faith that God has dealt to each of you." The context is that of self-evaluation. Do we understand our individual assignment within the Body of Christ? What gifts have we been given, what functions? Some of us will say we do not know. Others will give an answer based on others' estimates of us. Suppose we were to set aside half an hour to think soberly about what we can do and cannot do for the sake of the church. If we start by submitting everything to Christ and asking Him to change our minds and then proceed to concentrate faithfully on these words, we might be surprised to be shown that we have been wasting energy in doing things we are not suited to do, wasting time doing things that contribute nothing to the help of the church, and failing to do things we could do, things the Spirit of God brings to the mind that is directed to Him.

The Eastern art of meditation is not, I believe, similar to Christian meditation, but perhaps one lesson at least could be learned from it: that of assuming a special posture. I am not recommending any particular one, but any posture in which one can be both quiet and alert would be a good one. Closing the eyes has generally been considered a good way to pray because it screens out some of the distractions.

Do not try to "think about nothing." "Set your mind," Paul says, not, "Empty your mind." Set it on Christ, not on earthly things. One phrase from God's Word can be taken and repeated quietly, asking that we may be given ". . . the spiritual powers of wisdom and vision, by which there comes the knowledge of him." It was a phrase from the first chapter of Ephesians that I thought about this morning: "measured by His strength." It is helpful for me to start with the Word, expecting God to direct and control my thoughts within that context, leading me to others as He chooses. There will of course be spaces for listening.

Those who work with alcoholics sometimes tell them *not* to think. This is good advice in some circumstances. The mind can brood on matters that are of no help, as I know very well, though not in the context of alcoholism. I sometimes find myself turning something over and over mentally in the early hours of the morning, long before my alarm clock beeps. That is a bad time to indulge in thinking, first because it is the time for sleeping and second because there is nothing I can do about whatever it is at that hour anyway. Someone is sure to object here: "But I do my most creative thinking at two o'clock in the morning! I write poetry, plan menus, prepare a lecture, decide what investments I will make." The kind of thinking I refer to is the destructive kind—anxiety-producing thinking, taking thought for the morrow in the manner forbidden by Jesus; or that most deadly kind of all, brooding over bad memories. An alcoholic is in trouble the minute he allows himself to think about a drink. Sometimes it is dangerous for him to allow himself to think at all because that one thought will take precedence, so he is advised to get up and do something instead.

The transformation of the mind produces a transformed vision of reality. What the world calls "real" will lose its clarity. What it calls "unreal" will gain clarity and power.

Reading of men such as the apostle John or Saint Francis of Assisi or François de Fénelon, the unrenewed mind says "This man can't be real," forgetting that holiness is very real indeed. Holiness is, in fact, vastly more real, vastly more human than unholiness, being very much closer to what God created us to be.

What the world sees as real is one thing. What is real to the clearer eye of faith is quite another. So-called realism in literature usually treats evil as though it were the only reality and good as though it were fantasy. It concentrates on the ash can and the outhouse in the backyard, ignoring the rose bush in the front yard, which is certainly as real as they are. It is true that the bad characters in novels are often more believable than the good ones. Satan is the best drawn of Milton's characters, says C. S. Lewis. His explanation is this:

> Heaven understands Hell and Hell does not understand Heaven. . . . To project ourselves into a wicked character, we have only to stop doing something, and something which we are already tired of doing; to project ourselves into a good one we have to do what we cannot and become what we are not.

Christ calls us to do that (what we cannot), and to be that (what we are not). He is asking us to walk on water. Peter succeeded in doing that, but only for a few steps, only for those seconds when his gaze was locked on Christ's, his mind set, as it were, on "things above." But when he looked around, he sank.

It is nothing short of a transformed vision of reality that is able to see Christ as more real than the storm, love more real than hatred, meekness more real than pride, long-suffering more real than annoyance, holiness more real than sin.

John, Saint Francis, and Fénelon, holy men in the strongest sense, were deeply aware of their own sin.

"If we claim to be sinless, we are self-deceived and strangers to the truth," wrote the first.

The young Francis spent hours in anguished prayer in a grotto near his town, confessing and bewailing his sins. His face would be drawn with misery, until one day he came out in peace, knowing that God had forgiven him.

"We are amazed at our former blindness as we see issuing forth from the depths of our heart a whole swarm of shame-

ful feelings, like filthy reptiles crawling from a hidden cave,"
Fénelon wrote to a lady in 1690.

It is the man who is most realistic about his own need who
is most likely to turn from it to the shining reality of a savior.
Evil is never a reality in itself. That is, it has no existence
apart from the good, of which it is a corruption. Hell has no
light. It is murky. Therefore, the more clearly we apprehend
the nature of evil, the greater our revulsion and the more
wholeheartedly we turn from it and welcome the true. This
is what makes real men and real women, not the poor self-
indulgence that passes for honesty today when people
"share" their worst attitudes in order to get, not forgiveness,
but merely common sympathy and consent.

There is an admission of imperfection, foible, or "problem" that is not the same as genuine confession of sin. Instead, it smacks of the wish to be one with the crowd rather
than one with Him whom the world hated. Jesus spoke again
and again to His disciples of the hatred they would experience if they were true to Him:

> The world cannot hate you; but it hates me for exposing
> the wickedness of its ways.

> If the world hates you, it hated me first, as you know well.
> If you belonged to the world, the world would love its
> own. . . . Remember what I said: "A servant is not greater
> than his master." As they persecuted me, they will persecute
> you; they will follow your teaching as little as they have fol-
> lowed mine.

We need to be careful lest our eagerness to expose our
inner darkness becomes an exhibition or even a celebration
that will gain for us acceptance with those who really do love
darkness rather than light. The man who resolutely turns

from darkness to light will not have much popular support. The truth teller, as Socrates predicted long ago, will have his eyes gouged out. So it has been. So it will always be. We don't gouge eyes out nowadays, not in civilized society. We merely tell the man who turns from the broad road to the narrow that he is hung up, not in touch with his feelings, a do-gooder, a party pooper, holier than thou—any label that will exonerate the rest of us of the responsibility of being Christ-like. We pity his naiveté, his narrowness, his unreality, never suspecting that there could be in our midst a few whose *minds are set* on things above because their lives are hid with Christ.

> Who that for one moment has the least descried Him,
> Dimly and faintly, hidden and afar,
> Doth not despise all excellence beside Him,
> Pleasure and powers that are not and that are—
> Ay, amid all men bear himself thereafter
> Smit with a solemn and a sweet surprise,
> Dumb to their scorn, and turning on their laughter
> Only the dominance of earnest eyes?

A renewed mind has an utterly changed conception, not only of reality, but of possibility. A turn away from the kingdom of this world to the Kingdom of God provides a whole set of values based not on the human word, but on Christ's. Impossibilities become possibilities.

The worldly mind says, "Look, I'm human. Don't expect me to love that woman, not after what she did to my family. It's impossible."

The word of Christ is, "Love your enemies. Do good to them that hate you." This is indeed impossible, as it was impossible for Peter to walk on the sea, until he obeyed the command. The mind made over from within begins to think Christ's thoughts after Him.

I have found it necessary sometimes deliberately to refuse thoughts of what someone has done to me and to ask for help to dwell on what Christ has done for that person and wants to do for him and for me, for I am sure that my treatment of people depends on how I think about them. This hymn is often a helpful prayer to pray:

> May the mind of Christ my Savior
> Live in me from day to day,
> By His Love and pow'r controlling
> All I do and say.

When Paul went to visit the Corinthians, a church greatly in need of correction and purifying, he went "... weak, nervous, and shaking with fear," but with one resolve: to "... think of nothing but Jesus Christ—Christ nailed to the cross." It has helped me tremendously in facing a dreaded meeting with someone to take Paul's resolve, seeking to see that person only in the context of the cross. This simple method brings the imagination into play. Imagination is a power given us surely in order to enable us to enter into another's experience. Christ knows and loves the person and will transform my mind so that I see him as I could not have seen him before: loved, forgiven, redeemed. In this way, by the offering up of mind and imagination, I take my stand beneath the cross of Jesus. There things look very different from the way they look to the lonely self. Thus the only reality that the self would be able to see grows dimmer as the bright reality that can be seen by faith grows brighter.

This is new vision. The deliberate decision to think Christ's thoughts by allowing Him to remold the mind leads to a different way of seeing, which in turn leads to a different way of behaving toward others.

". . . Let your behaviour change, modelled by your new mind. This is the only way to discover the will of God and know what is good, what it is that God wants, what is the perfect thing to do."

One of my husband's great gifts is friendliness. He meets people easily and quickly puts them at ease. I don't. He helps me by example, and I am learning, but I also need his word. Recently he spoke to me about not having been as friendly as I should have been to a stranger. My immediate response to his remark was anger. That particular stranger happened to be a young person who stopped me in a hotel and addressed me by a nickname used only by my family and old friends. My annoyance showed, Lars said, in spite of my having smiled, greeted her, and expressed an interest in what she was doing. Lars gave me a brief lecture. Nothing I didn't already know. *Why should he lecture* me, I was thinking. He *has revealed impatience with people at times. And besides—that girl had no business. . . .*

My reaction was "real." It was honest, that is, it certainly was what came to mind first. I said aloud none of the things I was thinking, but what I was thinking was in the old pattern, not the new, not the mind of Christ. "Reality" is often evil. There is a common belief that a frank expression of what one naturally feels and thinks is always a good thing because it is "honest." This is not true. If the feelings and thoughts are wrong in themselves, how can expressing them verbally add up to something good? It seems to me they add up to three sins: wrong feeling, wrong thought, wrong action.

I knew my thoughts toward this girl were wrong to begin with, and my thoughts as Lars was exhorting me were much worse. The Holy Spirit reminded me of the truth: let God remold your mind. Set your mind on heavenly things.

Think Christ was the new thought that came. Where did it come from? Not from me. Not from a secular mind-set. The Holy Spirit reminded—*re*-minded—me.

"He who refuses correction is his own worst enemy, but he who listens to reproof learns sense."

"Lord, help me to face the truth of what Lars is saying to me, instead of blocking it out by self-defense," I prayed.

The natural mind prefers argument to obedience, solutions to truth. Its immediate response, when the truth is presented, is no. No way. It refuses to be nailed by the truth.

By "thinking Christ" I felt my resistance to the truth of Lars's words dissipate. The retorts I had thought of making died on my tongue. Submission to the authority of Christ brings authority over the self.

The longing for unity characterizes the renewed mind. No sincere Christian can happily accept divisions in the Body of Christ. When they arise because of envy, jealousy, party spirit, competitiveness, resentment, or the desire for recognition (and these are the causes of most fission), they reveal the old mind-set. The writers of the epistles repeatedly urge believers to think alike, to be of one mind, of the same mind, united in mind. How can we be otherwise if we have, in fact, the mind of Christ?

It is amazing how frequently things that are called disagreements prove, upon examination, to be simple dislike. "I don't agree with you" often means nothing more than "I don't like what you say." The Pharisees, famous for their knowledge of the law, claimed to disagree with Jesus. His replies showed up their disagreements to be hatred of the truth. Before we open our mouths to protest, we might consider carefully the possibility that we disagree only because agreement will cost us something, will inconvenience us, will be inimical to our vested interests. A case in point as I write is the refusal of Canadian air-traffic controllers to allow

United States flights to use Canadian airspace. The firing of our controllers, they claimed, made all United States flights "unsafe." This lasted two days and then, with no change at all in the situation in our control towers, they relented and permitted use of their airspace. Their disagreement, ostensibly founded on a real reason, became agreement without the "reasons" having changed a whit.

The democratic process, when it comes to voting in the church (for a new pastor, the purchase of a new lot, the renovation of the church kitchen, or the selection of deacons, elders or vestry) just as much as in the political realm, probably depends far more on taste than on thought. People either like things or they don't like them and would rather avoid the real labor of thinking. They have had so little practice in it that they are quite unable to distinguish between reason and personal preference.

The lack of practice is not the only explanation of this inability. Rejection of authority reduces everything to matters of taste. Where there is no absolute, there is only fashion. This is a serious thing, and one that Christians must criticize with the mind of Christ. How do we think about current issues: starvation, environmental crisis, the armament question, and the many issues created by the dehumanizing that results from what we might call "technolatry" (issues such as divorce, abortion, the desexualization of society, homosexuality, genetic engineering)?

Most of us feel utterly helpless in the face of all the horrors we see about us. Let us not lose perspective. It is in the context of the world as seen in Scriptures—a world created and upheld by God, a world corrupted but yet to be redeemed—that we must look at the news. We must activate our God-given understanding that there are invisible forces at work.

"For our fight is not against any physical enemy: it is

against organizations and powers that are spiritual. We are up against the unseen power that controls this dark world, and spiritual agents from the very headquarters of evil. Therefore you must wear the whole armour of God. . . ."

We are not limited in the usual sense to what one person can do. The Lord and His hosts fight for us.

"Weak men we may be, but it is not as such that we fight our battles. The weapons we wield are not merely human, but divinely potent to demolish strongholds; we demolish sophistries and all that rears its proud head against the knowledge of God; we compel every human thought to surrender in obedience to Christ."

We must apply these words to our own thinking, first of all. In every one of us are sophistries—pretensions, arguments that sound good but are misleading, and what Romano Guardini calls "afflictions of the heart that have assumed intellectual proportions."

Dr. Charles Stanley, pastor of the First Baptist Church in Atlanta, shows how strongholds develop. They begin with a thought. One thought becomes a consideration. A consideration develops into an attitude, which leads then to action. Action repeated becomes a habit, and a habit establishes a "power base for the enemy," that is, a stronghold. When we find ourselves wondering why we continue to do a thing we despise, here is the explanation. The enemy has made use of an area of weakness as his power base, and he hits us again and again. The only weapons adequate to deal with such strongholds are those that are mighty through God. They are spiritual weapons.

The one who has the mind of Christ does not necessarily *understand* all mysteries. He is willing, in fact, to stand in strong opposition to whatever rears its proud head against the knowledge of God, no matter what his opponents may say, no matter whether or not he can successfully refute their arguments. Maturity is the ability to carry the unanswered question in faith, holding to the Word by which we live.

A woman who had been viciously attacked publicly for something she had written on a particularly unpopular truth said to me, "Elisabeth, I can't answer them. I don't know what to say to some of their arguments, but I'm not afraid of them, because I know I'm right." It is a delicate business to take this stand, because the danger of bigotry lurks just around the corner, but the man whose eye is single for the glory of Another can be trusted.

Paul gave the young Timothy specific instructions about church order: the conduct of deacons, women, elders, and widows; no doubt these were explosive issues in his day as well as in ours. Paul knew well how hard it would be for Timothy if he took a firm stand. Nevertheless he said:

> This is what you are to teach and preach. If anyone is teaching otherwise, and will not give his mind to wholesome precepts—I mean those of our Lord Jesus Christ—and to good religious teaching, I call him a pompous ignoramus. He is morbidly keen on mere verbal questions and quibbles, which give rise to jealousy, quarrelling, slander, base suspicions, and endless wrangles: all typical of men who have let their reasoning powers become atrophied and have lost grip of the truth.

The disciple who means to compel every one of his thoughts to surrender in obedience to Christ would do well to test himself by asking:

1. Whose glory do I seek?
2. Is this for or against the knowledge of God?

3. Am I giving my mind to wholesome precepts?

4. Am I morbidly keen on mere verbal questions and quibbles?

5. Is it more important to me to understand than to obey?

6. Is it more important to me to know than to believe?

7. Will one side of the question inconvenience me?

8. Do I reject a particular truth because it will inconvenience me?

There is no end to the sophistries we are capable of substituting for clear thinking. Pragmatism (it's right if it works for me), technical feasibility (science has found a way to do it, so let's do it), relevance (I can "relate" to this), comfort (I feel comfortable with this), happiness (I feel happy about this), moderation (I certainly don't want to go to extremes), obligation (I owe this to myself), responsibility (it's *my* life), and so on.

Suppose we were to take the subjects of justice, human rights, abortion, divorce, masculinity and femininity. If we first put down on paper all the currently popular opinions about them and then asked the questions that I suggest, might we find answers in Scripture that would be quite revolutionary?

On justice: does it always mean, for the Christian, equality? Jesus told the story of a man who hired laborers at different times of the day and paid them all the same wage at the end of the day. Those who had been hired first grumbled at the amount paid ("Hey, how come those guys . . . ?") although it was exactly the amount agreed upon. The farmer had a right to be generous if he chose. Jesus shows in this story the meaning of "The last shall be first and the first last." "Is that fair?" we ask, but we are asking the wrong question. His emphasis was always on purity of heart and on love, rather than on law. He penetrated to the secrets of the hearts that were asking the questions and found in them strongholds of resistance to the truth.

On human rights: how many protesters would there be in the march if it were limited to those who had first given up their rights to themselves?

On abortion: which arguments in its favor would stand if the thing disposed of were called a baby instead of "tissue" or "the product of conception"? Are we permitted to ask whether it is a human being? Is our answer from God or from man?

On divorce: how many would seek one if it was the happiness of the other they desired above their own?

On masculinity and femininity: how many discussions about roles, equality, and personhood would grind to a halt if sexuality were seen not as a biological question, but as a theological one, a glorious mystery of two complementary beings who bear the image of the invisible God?

If we take each question, doctrine, problem straight into the presence of Christ, who *is* the Way, the Truth, and the Life, and ask, "Which way to the Kingdom of Heaven?" the answer will be there.

The disciple who honestly seeks to let God remold his mind will direct his energies not to sorting out the exceptions, loopholes, or fine points of law, but to a total surrender of obedient love. Then, with his heart open to the Spirit of God, he will be in a position to learn wisdom. The prayer of such a man or woman will be:

> Teach me, O Lord, the way set out in thy statutes,
>   and in keeping them I shall find my reward.
> Give me the insight to obey thy law
>   and to keep it with all my heart;

Make me walk in the path of thy commandments
    for that is my desire.
Dispose my heart toward thy instruction
    and not toward ill-gotten gains;
Turn away my eyes from all that is vile,
    grant me life by thy word.

The disciplined Christian will be very careful what sort of counsel he seeks from others. Counsel that contradicts the written Word is ungodly counsel. Blessed is the man that walketh not in that.

The power of God is manifest not in the wisdom of the wise (the philosopher? the scientist? the critic? the psychiatrist?) nor in the prudence of the prudent (the politician? the successful businessman? the tax advisor?) but in *Christ*—Christ nailed to a cross. What could appear more utterly useless and foolish to the world than that? Who could call on a man on a cross for wisdom? See where it got him!

But it was the cross that saved us. Christ was nailed to the cross in order that we might no longer live for ourselves, but for God. Isn't it just here, in our determination to get what we want when we want it, that so many of the problems for which we seek professional help begin? Might we not find our answer quickly if we bowed here first? I have. I know it's true. I also know there are those who will immediately object that this is too simplistic. To them I would answer simply that this is a book about Christian discipline. It is talking about starting points. It is directed to those who have already recognized their Master, and His Word is their frame of reference.

Paul warned Titus sternly to beware of men who turn their backs upon the truth: "... They talk wildly and lead men's minds astray. Such men must be curbed because they are ruining whole families. . . . They profess to acknowledge God, but deny him by their actions. Their detestable obstinacy disqualifies them for any good work."

Much sickness—physical, mental, and emotional—surely must come from disobedience. When the soul is confronted with an alternative of right or wrong and chooses to blur the distinction, making excuses for its bewilderment and frustration, it is exposed to infection. Evil is given the opportunity to invade the mind, the spirit, and the body, and the sick person goes off to an expert who will diagnose his trouble. Sometimes the patient knows well what his trouble is and for this very reason has not consulted the Lord, fearing what He will say: confess. Turn around. Quit that indulgence. Do not pity yourself. Forgive that person. Pay back what you owe. Apologize. Tell the truth. Deny yourself. Consider the other's well-being. Lay down your life.

The person is likely to choose a counselor who will listen "nonjudgmentally" to his story and perhaps make light of or dismiss as unwarranted whatever guilt feelings come to the surface. His interpretation of the secrets revealed may be more palatable than that which the patient would have found for himself on the pages of the Bible, for the Word ". . . cuts more keenly than any two-edged sword, piercing as far as the place where life and spirit, joints and marrow, divide. It sifts the purposes and thoughts of the heart. There is nothing in creation that can hide from him; everything lies naked and exposed to the eyes of the One with whom we have to reckon."

What human counselor, even with unexceptionable academic credentials, can, without the help of the living Word, pierce to the place where life and spirit divide?

To turn for help to one qualified to help, whose delight is in the law of the Lord, in whose law he meditates day and night, often leads out of confusion and darkness. The necessity of stating the case to another, the effort of sorting out all the factors, articulating them, presenting them in the light of day to another intelligence, and then looking at them reasonably together and praying through them one by one, can be a wonderfully enlightening experience.

God is not the author of confusion. His promise is:

> I will teach you, and guide you in the way you should go.
> I will keep you under my eye.
> Do not behave like horse or mule, unreasoning creatures,
> whose course must be checked with bit and bridle.
> Many are the torments of the ungodly;
> but unfailing love enfolds him who trusts in the Lord.
> Rejoice in the Lord and be glad, you righteous men,
> and sing aloud, all men of upright heart.

Two years ago my husband and I were faced with a very complicated business of buying a house, moving into it, and renting the house we moved out of. The timing seemed utterly impossible. We could not move out until the new place was ready; we could not promise prospective renters when our old house would be available (and we had a family desperately needing to move in). What to do? My thoughts had to be brought into captivity over that one. The taking of captives is not a gentle business. They don't want to come. But Christ is Master in our lives, which included housing difficulties, so thoughts simply had to be corralled. There seemed no way out of the tangle; and the minute I thought I had the fugitives safely captured, they would find another escape route, and off they would go.

Lars and I laid the whole thing before the Lord as completely as we could. We prayed for all the people on whom our decisions depended and for those who depended on our decisions, asking the Lord to provide for them as well as for us and to make clear to us what we should do. Then we set about doing what seemed reasonable and possible, one step at a time, trusting God to do what seemed beyond reason and impossible (which was most of it!). He answered our prayers. Now we find ourselves in another situation, similar, but even more complicated. Lars is away, and as I was praying alone yesterday, along the same lines we had prayed together two years ago, I picked up a Bible and "cracked" it at random. At once my eye fell on a note I had written in the margin of Psalm 18, "Praying for renter," and the date, which was within exactly a week of being two years from yesterday. ". . . My God will lighten my darkness. . . . The way of God is perfect, the Lord's word has stood the test. . . ." I wrote ditto marks in the margin under "Praying for renter," with a new date. I was encouraged to trust, bringing my disobedient thoughts—that is, my doubts and fears—into captivity. (Later note: we found renters, at exactly the right time.)

Are we eager to have a disciplined mind? We can readily test what sort we have by looking at biblical descriptions of the two kinds.

The carnal mind:

dulled	Luke 21:34 NEB
reprobate	Romans 1:28 KJV
depraved	Romans 1:28 NEB
set on the flesh	Romans 8:7 RSV
hostile to God	Romans 8:7 RSV
inevitably opposed to the purpose of God and neither can nor will follow His laws for living	Romans 8:7 PHILLIPS
sees no further than natural things	Romans 8:5 YOUNG CHURCHES

outlook formed by the lower nature, and that spells death	Romans 8:5 NEB
hard as stone	Ephesians 4:18 NEB
insensitive, blindfold in a world of illusion	Ephesians 4:18 YOUNG CHURCHES
set on earthly things	Philippians 3:19 NEB
bursting with futile conceit	Colossians 2:19 NEB
inflated by an unspiritual imagination, pushing his way into matters he knows nothing about	Colossians 2:18 RSV
tainted	Titus 1:15 NEB
diseased	Titus 1:15 YOUNG CHURCHES

The mind obedient to Christ shows a very different set of characteristics:

vigilant	Luke 21:36 PHILLIPS
sympathetic	Acts 17:11 PHILLIPS
ready	Acts 17:11 KJV
eager	Acts 17:11 NEB
humble	Philippians 2:5–9; Colossians 3:12 YOUNG CHURCHES
spiritual	Romans 8:6 NEB
reaches out after things of the spirit	Romans 8:6 YOUNG CHURCHES
life	Romans 8:6 NEB
peace	Romans 8:6 NEB
just	Ephesians 4:24 NEB
devout	Ephesians 4:24 NEB
sound	2 Timothy 1:7 KJV
self-discipline	2 Timothy 1:7 NEB
modesty	James 3:13 NEB

Of the wisdom that is not from above James says it is "earth-bound, sensual, demonic." It harbors bitter jealousy and selfish ambition, with which come disorder and evil of every kind.

The wisdom from above, on the other hand, ". . . is in the first place pure; and then peace-loving, considerate, and open to reason; it is straightforward and sincere, rich in mercy and in the kindly deeds that are its fruit."

The Christ-like mind counts for nothing what the world holds dear and holds as all-important what the world counts for nothing. I have been a Christian for nearly half a century, but I have a long way to go. When I am faced with a decision of any kind, if I examine my heart and mind, I nearly always find many characteristics of the unrenewed mind and only faint suggestions of the renewed. Am I vigilant? Sometimes. But just let me try to pray early in the morning or keep my mind on it when someone else is leading in prayer. The minute I think I've found a little generosity, I see that it applies only to my attitude toward certain people, not at all toward anybody who might be trying to do me in. If I detect, once in a blue moon, what looks like a minute dash of humility (and what am I doing "detecting" it anyway?), somebody sends me a review of one of my books, such as the recent one that ended up by suggesting that "some readers would say that this book is based on a superficial look at Scripture." Or I hear an account of a talk I am supposed to have given—misrepresented, misquoted, quoted out of context, misunderstood, or damned with faint praise—and I am undone. Do I reach out after the things of the Spirit? Well, sometimes. "Lord, thou knowest all things. Thou knowest that I love thee." My heart *is* hungering and thirsting for righteousness. Peace of mind? Yes, nearly always, except when I get home after a long trip and find the pileup of work on the desk.

If I am to love the Lord my God with *all* my mind, there will not be room in it for carnality, for pride, for anxiety, for the love of myself. How can the mind be filled with the love of the Lord and have space left over for things like that?

When I uncover them, I can only pray, "Lord, forgive me. I offer to You again my body as a living sacrifice, asking You to accept it as an act of worship and to continue Your holy work of transforming my mind from within, that I may more worthily glorify You. For Jesus' sake."

Throughout our earthly lives, it is always at the point of need—that moment of crisis when we cast about for some solution or answer or even some escape—that the opportunity is offered to us to *choose*. We will accept either the solutions, answers, and escapes that the world offers (and there are always plenty of those), or the radical alternative shown to the mind attuned to Christ's. The ways of the world exalt themselves against God. They sometimes look rational and appealing to the most earnest disciple, but Christ says to us then what He said to His disciples long ago, when many of them had already given up in disgust, "Do you also want to leave me?" If we answer as Peter did, "Lord, to whom shall we go? Your words are words of eternal life," our rebel thoughts are captured once more. The way of holiness is again visible. The disciple steps forward through the narrow gate.

NINE

The Discipline of Place

A FRIEND called me one day, on the telephone, with a question that made me think along new lines.

"Ron and I have not been very happy with the sermons we've been getting lately. I hardly know what to say to the minister when we come out of church and shake hands. But what bothers me most is how to honor him. Doesn't the Bible tell us to honor all men?"

It does. But what a quaint question for a modern young woman to ask. Honor? Who thinks of honor nowadays? We're all equal. We introduce ourselves by first names only; we neglect to use titles for people who would once have been considered our superiors; and the honor system in schools seems to have fallen on very hard times. I am not sure whether Boy Scouts still swear by "Scouts' honor" anymore, but the whole country was shaken recently when 13,000 air-traffic controllers broke an oath by striking. Some of the strikers may have had moments of misgiving, considering what the oath really meant, but the fact is that they struck, agreeing that their desires for a thirty-two hour week and a minimum of $30,642 per year superseded the oath they had signed. *Time* magazine, in reference to that fact, quoted William Murray, Britain's solicitor general in the eighteenth century: "No country can subsist a twelve-month where an oath is not thought binding, for the want of it must necessarily dissolve society."

The Bible tells us to give "due honor" to everyone. *Due*

means "owed, payable"; that is, it is not something above and beyond the call of duty, but something obligatory, just like bills, tolls, or taxes. It means also as much as is required, as "due care," or "in due time."

It has nothing to do with our feelings about ourselves or others, the air-traffic controllers notwithstanding.

"Discharge your obligations to all men; pay tax and toll, reverence and respect, to those to whom they are due. Leave no claim outstanding against you, except that of mutual love. . . ."

Here we must emphasize strongly that the disciple stands alone before God, facing his obligation primarily to God Himself. God will not ask him whether the other party fulfilled his part of the bargain. God asks only for a pure heart. It is easy enough to exonerate ourselves on the basis of the other party's (a person's, an institution's, a society's) failure to live up to its obligation, but a disciple's obedience is not contingent. "Leave no claim outstanding against *you*" is the individual's sole concern. There is no requirement that we make sure others pay us.

Honor means "respect, high regard, recognition of worth." A Christian sees all men as made in the image of God. All are sinners, too, which means that the image is marred, but it is a divine image nonetheless, capable of redemption and therefore to be held in honor.

One source of confusion is the definition of *respect. Respect* means "reverence under God," first of all; that is, a proper appreciation for the person God has made for the very reason that God made him. But the Bible says that God is "no respecter of persons," which means that He has no favorites. In the same sense James says we are inconsistent and judging by false standards if we "have respect," that is, if we play favorites, as when we pay special attention to the man who wears fine clothing.

To discriminate against someone for *false* reasons is wrong. In a place of worship both the well-dressed man with gold rings and the poor man in shabby clothes are to be welcomed. This is a Christian obligation. The rich man who comes in shabby clothes, however, illustrates another side of the coin of respect. Jesus told a story about a man who was thrown out into the dark, where there was weeping and grinding of teeth, because he appeared at a wedding improperly dressed. Of course the point Jesus was making in that story was not primarily one of respect, but the truth is there. Refusing the appropriate clothing (which, I am told, was customarily provided by the host to those who could not afford it) was an offense. The rich who assume shabbiness when they could well afford to dress *respect*ably are guilty of another form of favoritism: reverse snobbism.

I know I am skating on very thin ice to bring up the question of dress, since it has, for several decades, been considered by most Christians as of very minor importance or of absolutely no importance since God looks on the heart. But I believe it is worth reconsidering in terms of respect. Is it not an indication of my regard for another person's worth when I am willing to "dress up"—for a job interview, for example; for a special guest I am entertaining; for a social event to which I feel honored to have been invited? Is it not a sign of a performer's respect for his audience and of the audience's for the performer, when they dress for the occasion? It may be scorned as a form of pride ("who are you trying to impress?"), but it may be genuine humility of the same sort that would prompt one to polish the silver, get out the beautiful tablecloth, and have candlelight and flowers for someone greatly loved. The attitude of students, I have noticed, is strongly influenced by a professor's dress, as well as his manner.

A second reason for confusion in the matter of respect, in addition to that over the definition, is the current notion that everyone deserves tit-for-tat equality. This is one of the excesses of democracy, which ought not to be confused with Christianity. The truth is that not everybody has a right to everything. A child has the right to be taken care of. An adult has not. An adult has the right to vote, get married, be taxed. A child has not.

The key word, which will help us to understand some enormously important distinctions, is *due*. When Peter tells us to give due honor to everyone, he then goes on to specify three different ways of obeying that command: "... love to the brotherhood, reverence to God, honour to the sovereign." We have already noted that that which is due is that which is owed. It is fitting, proper, suitable to that particular person. Different kinds of honor and respect are suitable to different people, and in discriminating we actually do them honor. Nothing illustrates this more clearly than the wedding of Prince Charles and Lady Diana. By virtue of Charles's being a prince and the heir to the throne of England, the pomp and splendor of that wedding were due him. It was owed, fitting, proper, as much as was required and expected. That our expectations were fulfilled was a source of great joy. The faces of the crowds testified eloquently to this.

Honor is given. It is not taken. Had Prince Charles himself demanded the elaborate ceremony against the will of the monarch or the people, there would have been no joy in it whatsoever. He did not demand it—his position demanded it. This is essential in our understanding of the duty to honor one another. We must consider another's position before God.

Duty is another helpful word. It means simply "what is

due (as in customs duties which must be paid), any action necessary in or appropriate to one's occupation or position, a sense of obligation."

Hundreds of thousands waved flags, clapped, and cheered as the royal coach passed by. Elegantly uniformed horsemen rode splendidly caparisoned horses. Thus appropriate honor was tendered to the prince and princess, but they in their turn honored the crowd by nodding, smiling, waving, and appearing several times on the balcony of Buckingham Palace to acknowledge their subjects' acclaim. This response was their way of honoring the crowd.

Honor has to do with pride—pride in the truest, noblest sense of recognition of divine assignment. "Give pride of place to one another in esteem," says Paul to the Romans. Isak Dinesen comes closest to expressing what this means in her *Out of Africa:*

> The barbarian loves his own pride, and hates, or disbelieves in, the pride of others. I will be a civilized being, I will love the pride of my adversaries, of my servants, and my lover; and my house shall be, in all humility, in the wilderness a civilized place.
>
> Love the pride of God beyond all things, and the pride of your neighbor as your own. The pride of lions: do not shut them up in zoos. The pride of your dogs: let them not grow fat. Love the pride of your fellow-partisans, and allow them no self-pity.
>
> Love the pride of the conquered nations, and leave them to honor their father and their mother.

To love the pride of others requires a generous spirit. A small-spirited man will not be willing to see another receive credit or honor or position. All of us, I suppose, have sometimes grumbled inwardly seeing someone receive a place he did not deserve. "It is not fair. He is not qualified, whose idea was it to appoint him? How did he get on the board? How come I didn't?" The last question is the one that touches the deepest root of our unwillingness to honor another: our own pride, a wicked kind indeed that gives rise to jealousy. No doubt God must sometimes allow the "wrong" person to receive credit in order for us "right" ones to discover how full of pride we are.

Christianity teaches righteousness, not rights. It emphasizes honor, not equality. A Christian's concern is what is owed to the other, not what is owed to himself.

"Love your enemies; do good to those who hate you; bless those who curse you; pray for those who treat you spitefully. . . . Give to everyone who asks you; when a man takes what is yours, do not demand it back."

It is a long way from the old equal-rights law of an eye for an eye. Yet strangely, today, when equality is the alleged ideal, there is often reverse discrimination, where unfair advantage is given to those who were formerly at a disadvantage, for example, the criminal, the poor, ethnic groups, or women. In Old Testament times the Israelites were told that to be partial to or to favor the poor was a perversion of justice just as much as was subservience to the great.

". . . You shall judge your fellow-countrymen with strict justice . . . I am the Lord."

I am the Lord. It was enough of a reason for the people of Israel. We have even more reason, having seen the glory of God in the face of Jesus Christ, who became the Son of Man. Remembering Him, we honor all men.

Those whom we are specifically commanded to honor because they have been placed over us are civil authorities, parents, teachers, masters, and elders. Elders are worthy of double honor, or a double stipend. Those who suffer and work for us deserve honor.

Speaking of Epaphroditus, his fellow worker and comrade, Paul told the Philippians to welcome him with wholehearted delight and honor him, because "in Christ's cause he came near to death, risking his life to render me the service you could not give."

To the Thessalonians he wrote, "We beg you, brothers, to acknowledge those who are working so hard among you, and in the Lord's fellowship are your leaders and counsellors. Hold them in the highest possible esteem and affection for the work they do."

Mother Teresa of Calcutta honors the destitute and dying who lie on the streets of the city. She sees Christ in the sorriest scraps of humanity and with humility and love gathers them in to be cared for. No one who failed to recognize in them the divine image would do such a job.

Respect seems to be a hard thing for us to grasp in our present society. Many students in the seminary where I used to teach had what are called live-ins—situations in which, in return for housework or yard work, they are given a place to live, rent free. In talking with some of them, I have found that they have been offended at being treated as servants. They felt they should have been given a place as equals in the family. When I pointed out that the condition on which they were allowed to live there (some of the places are truly luxurious, on large ocean-front estates) was that they should serve, they seemed bewildered, having no conception of a servant's place.

A sense of place is important for a Christian. We cannot give honor duly—where it is due—without a sense of place. Who is this person, who am I in relation to him? We are people under authority at all times, owing honor and respect to a king or a president, to parents, to master, teacher, husband or boss, to ministers and elders and bishops, and of course always and most important, to Christ.

Another seminary student criticized a certain professor as being "unavailable." When questioned, he admitted that the professor delivered his lectures as scheduled and could be found in his office during the posted hours. He left the classroom immediately after lectures, however, and was not generally seen in the cafeteria, drinking coffee with students.

"But that's so wrong!" said the student.

"Wrong?"

"He doesn't relate. I mean, for one thing, he's the only professor I have that I don't call by his first name."

The young man had not the dimmest notion of honor or of giving pride of place.

Paul's advice to slaves illustrates a principle none of us should fail to understand:

> All who wear the yoke of slavery must count their own masters worthy of all respect, so that the name of God and the Christian teaching are not brought into disrepute. If the masters are believers, the slaves must not respect them any less for being their Christian brothers. Quite the contrary; they must be all the better servants because those who receive the benefit of their service are one with them in faith and love.

To be one in faith and love does not mean to be buddies, whether we are speaking of slaves and masters or students and professors. I tried to help the student to see that he needed to be concerned more to honor the professor by preserving a respectful distance than to stand on some misbegotten idea of student rights that entitled him to intimacy. His was the "right" to be taught, which right, like every other, has its limitations. The right to be a student is not the right to be a friend. If he becomes the professor's friend, that is a privilege.

Honoring those who are our rightful superiors by virtue of holding positions of authority over us takes the form of obedience. The servant is not greater than his lord, the student than his professor, the child than his parents. In each case, when obedience is offered first to Christ, obedience to the human superior will be rendered much easier. The standard of service ought also to be vastly improved.

"Do not offer merely the outward show of service, to curry favour with men, but, as slaves of Christ, do wholeheartedly the will of God. Give the cheerful service of those who serve the Lord, not men. For you know that whatever good each man may do, slave or free, will be repaid him by the Lord."

Gert Behanna, in her plea "Women Be Women!" (a talk given long before the women's liberation movement began), asks women who hate housework if they would be willing to iron a shirt or cook a meal for Jesus. To make any kind of service, no matter how menial, an offering to Him puts a whole new light on it.

The submissiveness of a wife to her husband is the appropriate form of honor that she pays him. She offers it just as she would offer it to Christ. In respecting her husband, she respects Christ—that is, she respects who he is in Christ. It is frequently argued that she owes him nothing if he is not fulfilling the special command issued to husbands: love your wives. This attitude produces a permanent stand-off. As long as she refuses to submit on the ground that he does not earn her respect, the husband, by the same logic, may refuse her his love, since she does not submit and therefore does not deserve it. Each has been given a particular command and a particular strength with which to meet the other more than halfway. In the case of the wife, her strength is what Peter calls an "... imperishable ornament, a gentle, quiet spirit. . . ." There is no calculating the power of such submission. It is even possible that an unbelieving husband will be won over without a word said when he sees the "chaste and reverent behavior" of his wife.

Is it possible to pay honor, like toll or taxes, to a cruel, abusive, unbelieving man? If everything in her recoils from her husband's injustice or hatred? If she fears suffering or other frightening consequences? The grace of God has proved through the centuries to be sufficient for countless "impossible" human circumstances. She may, through that grace, pay honor and respect to him *as to* the Lord, certain that although it is unmerited by and apparently lost on her husband, it is not lost on Christ. And Christ may draw the husband to faith because of her reverent behavior. Faith, not fear, should govern her. Try God! I would say.

Honor takes a form for the one *in* authority different from that for the one *under* authority. It takes an even greater humility, like that of Christ, who though rich beyond all telling, for the sake of poor sinners, became poor. He annihilated Himself and went down into death for us.

"Husbands, love your wives as Christ loved the Church." What an assignment. What an honor—for him to love her so, for her to be so loved. The husband is to pay honor to the wife's body specifically *because* it is weaker and because they are heirs together of [they share] the grace of life. Thus *honor* is understood to mean not only respect for superiority, but reverence under God for the *inferior,* which means "the one placed under." There is no room for tyranny here, no such thing as bullying, lording it over, bossing. It is a gracious humility that honors the weaker one.

To return to the prince's wedding—no one is surprised to

see the enthusiasm of the cheering crowds. *Of course* they will cheer. *Of course* thousands will willingly spend the night on the pavement in order to catch a glimpse of the coach and its resplendent occupants. But when the prince himself returns the honor by a gracious smile, those nearby who feel sure it is meant for them are "surprised by joy," and their hearts are filled to bursting with humble pride. The greater has honored the lesser. It is not only a royal obligation (noblesse oblige); it is commanded by God.

Masters are commanded to treat slaves with respect: ". . . Give up using threats; remember you both have the same Master in heaven, and he has no favourites."

Special honor is due to other "weak" ones who, like slaves, are not in positions of power. Widows who had no children or grandchildren were given special status or honor.

Children must receive due honor: "You fathers, again, must not goad your children to resentment, but give them the instruction, and the correction, which belong to a Christian upbringing." This is just. The rights of children include being cared for physically, spiritually, and mentally, but surely do not include the right to be heard in matters they know nothing about or to be treated as equals with parents and teachers. To grant them that right is to wrong them. It is dishonor, for it deprives them of liberty—the liberty to be children—and of justice—the just treatment of children. To honor them, then, is to grant them whatever privileges and responsibilities are justly due and can be properly exercised.

Our great model in this, as in all other aspects of the disciplined life, is Jesus. Honor was His very mode of existence. Just before He was crucified He prayed to His Father, referring to the completion of everything the Father had given Him to do as being the way in which He, Christ, had honored Him. He asked the Father to honor Him also in the Father's own presence, and He speaks of believers having done Him honor. While Jesus actually used the word *honor* in referring to the three ways in which it worked—His honoring the Father, the Father's honoring Him, and the believers' honoring Him—there is a fourth way: His honoring believers. It is implied throughout the prayer, in phrases such as:

> I have shown your self to the men whom you gave me from the world.
>
> Every message which you gave me I have given them.
>
> I am praying for . . . the men whom you gave me.
>
> I have sent them to the world just as you sent me.

Is there any honor to be compared, from our standpoint, to the Lord of Lords and King of Kings having stooped to lift us men up into the Godhead?

The measure of the humiliation of Christ is the measure of the honor that has been bestowed on us.

Notes in the Jerusalem Bible on Philippians 2 give this explanation:

> Christ, being God, had all the divine prerogatives by right. [He] "did not deem being on an equality with God as something to grasp" or "hold on to." This refers not to his equality by nature 'subsisting in the form of God', and which Christ could not have surrendered, but to his being publicly treated and honoured as equal to God which was a thing that Jesus (unlike Adam, Gn 3:5,22, who wanted to be seen to be like God) could and did give up in his human life.
>
> "He emptied himself": this is not so much a reference to the fact of the incarnation, as to the way it took place. What Jesus freely gave up was not his divine nature, but the glory

to which his divine nature entitled him, and which had been his before the incarnation, Jn 17:5, and which "normally" speaking would have been observable in his human body. . . . He voluntarily deprived himself of this so that it could be returned to him by the Father, cf. Jn 8:50,54, after His sacrifice.

No wonder, then, that Paul writes:

There must be no room for rivalry and personal vanity among you, but you must humbly reckon others better than yourselves. Look to each other's interest and not merely to your own.

Let your bearing towards one another arise out of your life in Christ Jesus. For the divine nature was his from the first; yet He did not think to snatch at equality with God [margin: yet he did not prize his equality with God], but made himself nothing, assuming the nature of a slave. Bearing the human likeness, revealed in human shape, he humbled himself, and in obedience accepted even death—death on a cross."

His giving up of the glory to which His divine nature entitled Him seems to me perhaps the most incredible part of His humiliation. His obedience enabled Him to do anything, anything at all that would please the Father, without thought of "how it would look." He who had known the ceaseless worship of angels came to be a slave to men. Preaching, teaching, healing the sick, and raising the dead were parts of His ministry, of course, and the parts we might consider ourselves willing to do for God if that is what He asked. He could be *seen to be God* in those. But Jesus also walked miles in dusty heat. He healed, and people forgot to thank Him. He was pressed and harried by mobs of exigent people, got tired and thirsty and hungry, was "tailed" and watched and pounced upon by suspicious, jealous, self-righteous religious leaders, and in the end was flogged and spat on and stripped and had nails hammered through His hands. He relinquished the right (or the honor) of being publicly treated as equal with God.

If you and I were asked to write the job description of a savior, what would go on the list? A careful look at what the will of the Father included for the Savior of the world will give us a clue to what a follower of His might be expected to do. We would hardly have expected Him to have to go to a village wedding, to be a dinner guest in many different kinds of homes, to take into His arms little children who were nothing but a nuisance to the disciples, or to heal a woman who was not one of the "lost sheep" of Israel.

I think of the job description, for example, of a missionary. My brother Dave (Howard) and I were discussing the number-one qualification. Dave has been connected with missions and missionaries in one way or another all his life, and he had no trouble setting flexibility at the top of the list. Humility was what I had thought of, but as we talked about it I saw that they really come to the same thing.

A missionary must be humble enough to be flexible. Nowadays young candidates are often so highly trained that they feel overqualified for the jobs that need to be done. Most mission stations are in desperate need of people who are willing to do anything that needs doing. It is fine to offer oneself for service, but the form of service must not be too narrowly defined. It is to minister, not to be ministered to, that we are sent.

I went to Ecuador to do Bible translation work, a job that certainly needs doing. But in order to do that, I had to start out by learning unwritten languages. To do that, I had to spend a lot of time with the people who spoke the language and who were not the least bit interested in Bible translation. To spend time with them, I had to do what they did, sit where they sat, eat what they ate, try hard to think what they thought (up to a point!). I also had to live. Living took a lot of time, under what were for me sometimes tough conditions. I needed a gasoline lamp, so I spent precious minutes reaming the generators or replacing the mantles or filling these lamps. "Missionary" work? Yes, necessarily.

I was not trained to do medical work, but when you find that you are the only person for miles around who is willing to get blood on her hands and sometimes her clothes, who knows how to give an injection or administer worm medicine, you end up doing just that. If you are going to have some semblance of civilized efficiency in your life, you introduce things like bed sheets, airstrips, screened windows, maybe a kerosene refrigerator. First thing you know, you are not sitting at a desk, filing language cards or trying to figure out how to put "In the beginning was the Word" into Quichua, but you're down on the floor, on your stomach, peering at the smoking wick of the refrigerator, trying to figure out what to do about it before everything rots in the tropical heat. Or you are washing sheets by hand or teaching somebody else how to do it. You are the foreman on the airstrip, hoping to keep twenty-five men and women happily swinging machetes for four hours in the hot sun (the sun bothers *you*, not them) and hoping that the result will be an airstrip that meets the missionary pilot's specifications.

The question arises fairly soon in a missionary's career (the same question that arises in any disciple's), "What is my 'place,' after all?"

What was Jesus' place? A servant. A slave. My bearing toward others arises out of my life in Him.

At first the missionary's position may be that of honoring those to whom he goes as the stronger honors the weaker, or the benefactor the beneficiary. But that will soon change. I was deeply aware of my position as alien, freak, and liability to the Indians. Helpless to know how to cope with the jungle itself, utterly ignorant and seemingly retarded with regard to the language, possessing nothing of much use to them, I was certainly not in a position of power. As we began to give them the Scriptures in their own language and they believed and started to obey them, they began to recognize our reason for being there and to look to us for guidance. This was a shift to a position of authority, soon to be followed by another, where we handed over the reins and learned to honor them no longer as weaker, but as spiritually responsible to God. Gracefully to relinquish one place and take up another, to continue to work with the growing church, but under its authority, requires a true and sharp assessment of one's place, as well as a single eye for God's glory.

I was helped toward this understanding by realizing that I was a clay pot. I saw a good many clay pots in Indian houses. They were very common; they were made out of stuff to be found in almost any stream and easily replaceable. What was in them was of much more interest than the pots themselves. This was what I was—common stuff, replaceable, but holding a "priceless treasure," the life of Jesus. Only as I lived that life would I be able to give pride of place to others in esteem.

Surely one of the joys of heaven will be the wholehearted acceptance of and thanksgiving for the place others have been given, for our concern there will no longer be place, honor, or rights for ourselves, but blessing and honor and glory and power to the Lamb who sits on the throne.

TEN

The Discipline of Time

Lover of All, I hold me fast by Thee,
Ruler of time, King of Eternity
There is no great with Thee, there is no small,
For Thou art all, and fillest all in all.

The newborn world swings forth at Thy command,
The falling dewdrop falls into Thy hand.
God of the firmament's mysterious powers
I see Thee thread the minutes of my hours.

AMY CARMICHAEL has beautifully bound together in her poem the two ancient concepts of time. One, expressed by the Greek word *chronos,* refers to "the minutes of our hours," or the notion of duration and succession. The other, *kairos,* is what Dr. James Houston calls "time evaluated," signifying instrumentation and purpose. "Man needs to see himself significant, in the light of events, of *kairos,* seeing himself hopefully in the context of a greater reality than his own temporality, of *chronos.*"

"I hold me fast by Thee, Ruler of time, King of Eternity" is the expression of faith that my temporality is understood only in the infinite context of eternity. Not even the tiny dewdrop lacks the care and attention of the Lover of all. Shall I then think of any detail of my earthly life, even so little a thing as a minute of one of my hours, as without meaning? How shall I answer to my Master for my time?

I was brought up to believe that it is a sin to be late. To cause others to wait for you, my parents taught us, is to steal from them one of their most precious commodities. Time is a *creature*—a created thing—and a gift. We cannot make any more of it. We can only receive it and be faithful stewards in the use of it.

"I don't have time" is probably a lie more often than not, covering "I don't want to." We *have* time—twenty-four hours in a day, seven days in a week. All of us have the same portion. "If the president can run the country on twenty-four hours a day, you ought to be able to get your room cleaned" is what one mother said to her teenage son. Demands on our time differ, of course, and it is here that the disciple must refer to his Master. What do You want me to do, Lord? There will be time, depend upon it, for *everything* God wants us to do.

When we are in the midst of great busyness, we hardly think of *kairos* and see *chronos* only as hours that are flying by faster than we can count. It is when things are quiet that we become aware of minutes that tick slowly by. Then we have opportunity, perhaps, to think of their deeper significance in the light of eternity.

This chapter is being written in quiet. It is especially blissful since it follows three rather rigorous weeks of travel in England—two thousand miles of it, many meetings, many different beds, countless cups of tea. I wasn't sure where I was when I woke in the morning. "Let's see—is it Tuesday? This must be Sheffield."

I dreamed last night that I was again in a meeting, listening to the two or three speakers who were to precede me, nervously turning over in my mind what I was going to say. Then it occurred to me in my dream that I need not give a talk at all. I could wake up if I chose, which I did, to my immense relief, finding nothing but a long, quiet day before me, in which I would not speak.

In fact, I would not even talk. I am alone in the *hytte*. No telephone will ring, no mail will arrive. There are long stretches of unmarked time—there is no alarm clock, no morning news to listen to, no specified time for meals since, on the days when Lars is here, he fishes. I am never sure whether the menu will include fish or what time we may sit down at the table. Lars goes off, sometimes overnight, to visit relatives and see the places where he grew up, while I stay alone. Hardly any cleaning or cooking is necessary. I have few choices of clothes to wear. It is bliss to "have time."

The sense of time is strangely altered here because of the duration of the daylight. It is June, and the sun seems reluctant to set at all. It hangs high in the western sky over the water, and when nighttime ought to be upon us, the sun has slipped only a little below the horizon, where it rolls along parallel to the line of low hills. I wake at midnight and go to stand by the picture window, looking over the fjord. The sky is lit with an eerie glow, like the foreboding luminosity of a storm-darkened afternoon. Not once have I had to light a lamp, so there is no "punctuation" for evening and morning.

Sunrise, noon, sunset, midnight. Sunday, Monday, Tuesday, and Wednesday. January, May, September. Winter, spring, summer, autumn. Easter, Thanksgiving, Christmas. These are the punctuation marks of time, and what a marvelous mercy that God divided light from darkness, "and the evening and the morning were the first day." Six days, then a day for rest. Moons that wax and wane. Seasons that come and go.

"For everything its season, and for every activity under heaven its time," wrote Qoholeth, the preacher of the book of Ecclesiastes. For birth, death, planting and uprooting, killing and healing, pulling down and building up, weeping and laughing, mourning and dancing, scattering stones and gathering them, embracing and refraining, seeking and losing, keeping and throwing away, tearing and mending. There are times for silence and speech, for love and hate, for war and peace.

"I have seen the business that God has given men to keep them busy. He has made everything to suit its time; moreover he has given men a sense of time past and future, but no comprehension of God's work from beginning to end."

Here is a recipe for boredom and cynicism. If life is nothing more than a meaningless string of minutes threaded on hours, with no comprehension of God's work from beginning to end, the hillbilly song says it all:

> Open the door and the flies come in,
> Shut the door and I'm sweatin' again
> Life gets tejus, don't it?

For the Christian, time is transfigured as we see it held in the love of God, created by and for Jesus Christ, to whom belongs the primacy over all created things and who existed before everything and holds everything together. We see the past as God's continuous action in man's history, giving him freedom to act, and the future as belonging also to Him and holding for us the hope of redemption. We are given the present within which to choose whom we will serve, knowing that this moment affects the next and we are accountable for it.

The ninetieth psalm expresses the human sense of time and its awesome swiftness and seriousness yet looks with hope at the timelessness of God and the promise of future gladness.

Before the mountains were brought forth ... thou art
  God....
in thy sight a thousand years are as yesterday....
they are like a dream at daybreak....
our years die away like a murmur
Seventy years is the span of our life,
eighty if our strength holds;
the hurrying years are labour and sorrow,
so quickly they pass and are forgotten....
Teach us to order our days rightly,
that we may enter the gate of wisdom....
Satisfy us with thy love when morning breaks,
that we may sing for joy and be glad all our days.
Repay us days of gladness for our days of suffering....

It is wonderfully stabilizing and quieting to recall some of the ways in which God's timing is seen in the great Bible stories. Events the world would dismiss as mere coincidence turn out to have been synchronized with utmost precision by the Ruler of time. When Abraham's servant went to find a wife for Isaac, he made the camels kneel by the well outside the city and was praying for guidance to the right girl. Before he finished praying, there she was.

When Ruth went to glean in the fields behind the reapers, it "happened" that she was in the strip that belonged to Boaz, and she appeared there just as he came out from Bethlehem. He became her "kinsman-redeemer."

The boy David, sent with provisions for his brothers who were soldiers, arrived at the encampment as the Philistine host was shouting the war cry. David ran to the ranks and was just in time to hear the giant of Gath, Goliath, thunder his challenge: "Here and now I defy the ranks of Israel. Give me a man, . . . and we will fight it out." And David, though only a youth, "ruddy and comely," defied him in the name of the Lord of Hosts and sank a stone from his slingshot into Goliath's forehead.

One verse in the second book of Kings tells of a strange and amazing stroke of "luck": "Year by year Moabite raiders used to invade the land. Once some men were burying a dead man when they caught sight of the raiders. They threw the body into the grave of Elisha and made off; when the body touched the prophet's bones, the man came to life and rose to his feet."

When Jesus told Peter and John to go and prepare the Passover, they were to find the house where He wanted to celebrate it by following a man carrying a water jar, whom they would meet as they entered the city. They found it exactly as He had said.

Philip's meeting with the Ethiopian minister of the treasury was arranged by the angel of the Lord, who got to Philip in time to send him to the Jerusalem–Gaza road in time to connect with a certain chariot in which a man happened to be reading a certain passage in a certain book that Philip happened to be able to explain to him. The man became a believer.

"My times are in thy hand . . ." has become a part of my life. When the Lord has left me in an agony of waiting over some decision, these words have put me at rest. His timing is always perfect, though it seldom seems so to me, for my temperament longs for previews of coming attractions.

"Wait for the Lord; be strong, take courage, and wait for the Lord" is the word I need many times.

After an evening meeting in which I had spoken about the timing aspect of the guidance of God, a woman said to me, "I know exactly what you mean. It's been my experience, too. When I had offered myself for missionary service, I expected God would show me at once where He wanted me. He didn't. I waited and prayed, and prayed and waited, desperate to know. *Why* didn't He tell me? *Why* must I wait? I had been trained as a dietician, but could not imagine that that would be of much use on the mission field. It was eighteen months after I had volunteered, eighteen months of importunate praying, when a missionary came to the Bible school to speak. At the very end of her talk, she said, 'And we ask your prayers that the Lord will send us a dietician for India.' Straightaway the Lord said, 'That's you, Gwen. Off you go!' and in six months I was in India."

"My times are in thy hands." Quite often they seem to be in other people's hands. When I wish for solitude and no interruptions, the phone rings, people come, mail arrives that demands immediate action. Do I imagine that the interruptions come as a surprise to the Lord? Are they not, just as much as the planned things, a part of the pattern of things that work together for good?

Flying in a small plane over Manitoba's vast farm country, one spring evening, I was fascinated by the beauty of the patterns created by the contour plowing. There were stripes in varied shades of earth and greenness, circles and swaths and curves for miles and miles on every side. But the most beautiful designs grew out of the interruptions—a tree here, a pond there, a hill, a rock, a river. The plowman had had to bend the line each time he passed one.

"Lord, when there are interruptions, it seems that the disposal of the time I had planned so well has slipped out of my hands. Help me then to remember that it has not slipped out of Yours. In Your hands, these unexpected things will be fashioned into an unexpectedly beautiful design."

The sum of our job here on earth is to glorify God. This

was the sum of Jesus' task as well. How did He do it? Shortly before He was crucified He said to His Father, "I have glorified thee on earth by completing the work which thou gavest me to do."

There were endless demands on Jesus' time. People pressed on Him with their needs so that He and His disciples had not leisure even to eat, and He would go away into the hills to pray and be alone. At times the disciples came to Him with reproach because He was not available when needed. There must have been, everywhere He went, those who wanted to be healed who could not get to Him because of the crowds, or who learned too late that Jesus of Nazareth was passing by, or who had no one to carry them to Him or to send to ask Him to come to them. How many "if only's" He must have left behind, how much more that He "could have" done. There must have been things, also, that Jesus Himself would have liked to do during those three packed years of His public ministry, but He was a man, with a man's limitations of time and space. Yet He took time to rest, withdrawing to the hills to pray alone and sometimes taking His disciples to lonely places where they were free of the crowds. Still He was able to make that amazing claim, "I have finished the work You gave me to do." This was not the same as saying He had finished everything He could possibly think of to do or that He had done everything others had asked. He made no claim to have done what He wanted to do. The claim was that He had done what had been *given*.

This is an important clue for us. The work of God is appointed. What was given to the Son to do was the will of the Father. What is given to us to do is also His will.

There is always enough time to do the will of God. For that we can never say, "I don't have time." When we find ourselves frantic and frustrated, harried and harrassed and "hassled," it is a sign that we are running on our own schedule, not on God's.

I wrote to a friend, telling her the things on my roster for which I needed her prayers. It was a long list, more than I felt I could possibly accomplish.

" 'Thy list be done' is what I'm praying for you these days," she wrote back. It is a good prayer for a disciple to pray. I am all for making lists of what needs to be done (and I am exhilarated by checking them off when finished!). But the lists must be reviewed daily with the Lord, asking Him to delete whatever is not on His list for us, so that before we go to bed it will be possible to say, "I have finished the work You gave me to do."

"*My* burden is light," Jesus said. It is the addition of burdens God never meant us to carry that weighs us down. Learn to say no. Many busy Christians find they must schedule "free" time—time to be quiet, to read books, to be with family. If they don't do this, the time is easily filled with the demands others make. There is nothing dishonest about telling someone, "I'm sorry. That evening is not open." If it has been set aside for quietness or for family, it is not open to other activities.

"My times," which are in God's hands, now happen to include for me rather a lot of traveling. Lars and I pray over the schedule, asking the Lord to give us wisdom in arranging the traveling and the time at home. It is not easy to know what to say to an invitation for an engagement eighteen months or more hence. We are cast on the Lord, who sees the end from the beginning, and we can only trust Him to guide us in our replies. Each year I try a little harder to be sensible, to leave space in between the trips for the other things I ought to do, and each year it seems more difficult to sort out the commitments. When we come home from a trip, it is often late at night. We unpack the suitcases and go to bed, resisting the temptation to make phone calls or open the mail. In the morning the routine begins: open mail, tear off all the stamps for the Iran missionary box at the church, read mail, sort it into piles—immediate reply (business letters, invitations, bills, and so on), delayed reply (friendly letters). Organize desk top, do the laundry, clean the house, buy groceries, answer the mail, bake bread, wash hair, visit mother, make phone calls. Try to write, think, read, and pray—before packing another suitcase.

Frustration is not the will of God. Of that we can be quite certain. There is time to do anything and everything that God wants us to do. Obedience fits smoothly into His given framework. One thing that most certainly will not fit into it is worry. Here are six reasons why:

1. Worry is totally fruitless. Have you ever succeeded in adding an inch where you wanted it, or subtracting one where you didn't want it, merely by being anxious? If you can't accomplish that by worrying, what *can* you accomplish?

2. Worry is worse than fruitless: it is disobedience. Note these commands:

Fret not.
Fear not.
Let not your hearts be troubled.
Be not dismayed.
Be of good cheer.

3. Worry is taking the not-given—for example, tomorrow. Tomorrow is not ours to worry about. We are allowed to

plan for tomorrow, but we are not allowed to worry about it. Today's troubles are enough of a burden. Jesus knew exactly what He was talking about when He said that.

4. Worry is refusing the given. Today's care, not tomorrow's, is the responsibility given to us, apportioned in the wisdom of God. Often we neglect the thing assigned for the moment because we are preoccupied with something that is not our business just now. How easy it is to give only half our attention to someone who needs us—friend, husband, or little child—because the other half is focused on a future worry.

5. Worry is the antithesis of trust. You simply cannot do both. They are mutually exclusive.

6. Worry is a wicked squandering of time (as well as energy).

Direct your time and energy into worry, and you will be deficient in things like singing with grace in your heart, praying with thanksgiving, listening to a child's account of his school day, inviting a lonely person to supper, sitting down to talk unhurriedly with wife or husband, writing a note to someone who needs it.

People wish they had more leisure time. The problem is not too little of it, but too much of it *poorly spent*. The Sunday papers, nearly all magazines, and nearly all television programs are an unconscionable waste of time.

Jesus calls us, "Come to me, all whose work is hard, whose load is heavy; and I will give you relief. Bend your necks to my yoke, and learn from me, for I am gentle and humblehearted. . . ."

How shall we come to Him? In faith first, for our salvation. No step can precede that one. But the one who has put his trust in the Lord must continue to come on a daily basis to learn from Him how to be gentle and humble hearted. Time management, a highly developed science today, begins for the Christian with time set aside for God. Other things cannot fall into a peaceful order if this is omitted.

The life of Daniel illustrates the discipline of time. He had a regular schedule for prayer. King Darius issued an ordinance that anyone who in the next thirty days offered a petition to any god or man other than himself would be thrown into a lions' pit.

We can imagine Daniel's perplexity. Should he alter his prayer time? Reduce the frequency? Eliminate prayer altogether? Choose a less conspicuous place? A casual posture?

His enemies were looking for a way to catch him, and of course they had no trouble finding it.

"When Daniel learnt that this decree had been issued, he went into his house. He had had windows made in his roof-chamber looking towards Jerusalem; and there he knelt down three times a day and offered prayers and praises to his God as his custom had always been."

He was an easy target, but saving his skin was not nearly so important to him as serving his God. Prayer was indispensable to that, so he was willing to let himself be caught.

Just a few words about the most important time of the day: that spent alone with the Lord.

1. Let it be a regular time. At least five days a week have a special time for solitude and silence. If you have never done it before, start with ten minutes. You will be surprised how quickly this goes, and you will soon need to plan for more.

2. Have a special place. Anywhere where you can be alone, even if it has to be a closet, bathroom, or the car in the garage.

3. Let your prayer include worship, thanksgiving, con-

fession of sin, petition (including one asking God to speak to you during your quiet time), and intercession (prayers for others). Lists of names of people to pray for are a great help for most of us. When people ask me especially to pray for them, I need to write down the names so I won't forget.

4. Keep a spiritual journal, noting lessons learned, Scriptures applied to a particular need, prayers answered. This is a great encouragement to faith.

5. Read a portion of the Bible in some ordered sequence. Three chapters per day and five on Sundays will take you through the whole Bible in a year. Some people like to read two chapters of the Old Testament and one in the New each day. Billy Graham reads from both Psalms and Proverbs daily, along with whatever other portion of the Bible he is in.

The best time for most people is early morning—not because most of us love jumping out of bed, but because it is the only time of day when we can be fairly sure of not being interrupted and because it is best to commune with God before you commune with people. Your attitude toward them will then arise out of your life in Him. Offering to God the first hour of the day is a token of consecration of all of our time.

ELEVEN

The Discipline of Possessions

ROSALIND GOFORTH, in her story of the life she and her husband led as missionaries in China, told of being robbed by bandits of everything they possessed. She wept.

"But my dear," her husband, Jonathan, chided. "They're only *things!*"

"So also none of you can be a disciple of mine without parting with all his possessions," was what Jesus said about things.

It is a stern condition. Few of us fulfill it literally.

I enjoy material things. In the *hytte,* primitive though it would seem to many Americans, we had plenty of comforts. There was a stainless-steel sink in the tiny kitchen, which lacked only faucets. It had a drain that ran into plastic containers that Lars emptied every few days. We had a bottled-gas stove on which we cooked and heated water in a big orange teakettle; all our hot water came from this source, to be used for both dishwashing and bathing. Water was collected in a large tank from the roof and carried into the house in a pail. The outhouse was first class—lace curtains at the window, pictures on the wall.

I am back home now, however, and appreciate more than ever a tiled bathroom and a kitchen sink with faucets. Hot water is an extravagant luxury, and I often thank God for it.

It usually takes loss or deprivation in some measure for most of us to count the blessings we so readily take for granted. The loss of material things is not to be compared with the loss of people we love, but most of us have experienced both, and it is things we are considering now.

I lost a year's language work at the end of my first year as a missionary.

Several years after my husband Jim died, I attended a performance at Lincoln Center, New York. When I took off my kid gloves later I saw that I had lost the diamond engagement ring he had given me. I went back immediately and searched through the rows of seats with a policeman and his flashlight, but the cleaning women had already done their vacuuming.

In Costa Rica I was relieved of my billfold when I laid it on the counter for a second and fished in my bag for my passport. The nimble travel agent on the other side of the counter (there was no one else anywhere near us) knew nothing about it and most solicitously helped me look for it.

I lost a New Testament with nineteen years' worth of notes in it.

My house has been robbed twice. The first time they got not only the replaceables, like the television, a radio, and a tape recorder, but all the heirloom sterling. When the second robbery occurred, I wondered why I had not put up a notice sooner: "This place has been cleaned out of the things you're looking for—it will hardly be worth the risk of breaking in." My friend Harriet Payson had a better idea. She put a little sign in her silver drawer, "God loves you."

Few of us are as well acquainted with the extremes that the apostle Paul knew: "I know what it is to be brought low, and I know what it is to have plenty. I have been very thoroughly initiated into the human lot with all its ups and downs—fullness and hunger, plenty and want." In whatever measure we have experienced these, the Lord has given us opportunity to learn the vital disciplines of possession.

The first lesson is that things are *given by God.*

"Make no mistake, my friends. All good giving, every perfect gift, comes from above, from the Father of the lights of heaven."

I often see, shining in the deep blue of the sky just before dawn, the morning star. At twilight the sea sometimes reflects the pale rose and daffodil colors of the sunset. At night I awaken to find the room flooded with moonlight reflected from the sea, from the glass top of my desk by the window, and from the mirror of the dressing table. Flying at thirty thousand feet, I have seen glorious light shining on the towers and castles of thunderheads. What a gift are these lights of heaven! The same Father who gives them also gives us all other good and perfect things.

It is God's nature to give. He can no more "help" giving than He can "help" loving. We can absolutely count on it that He will give us everything in the world that is good for us, that is, everything that can possibly help us to be and do what He wants. How can He not do this?

"He did not spare his own Son, but gave him up for us all; and with this gift how can he fail to lavish upon us all he has to give?"

The second lesson is that things are given us *to be received with thanksgiving.*

God gives. We receive. Animals do this, too, but more directly and simply than we do:

> ... The earth is full of thy creatures, beasts great and
> small ...
> All of them look expectantly to thee
> to give them their food at the proper time;
> what thou givest them they gather up;
> when thou openest thy hand, they eat their fill.

Because God gives us things indirectly, by enabling us to make them with our own hands (out of things He has made, of course), or to earn the money to buy them, or to receive them through someone else's giving, we are prone to forget that He gave them to us.

". . . What do you possess that was not given you? If then you really received it all as a gift, why take the credit to yourself?"

The taking of credit becomes an absurdity when we remember that not only the brains, abilities, and opportunities for achievement are gifts, but also the very air we breathe and the ability to draw it into our lungs.

We should be thankful. Thanksgiving requires the recognition of the Source. It implies contentment with what is given, not complaint about what is not given. It excludes covetousness. The goodness and love of God choose the gifts, and we say thank you, acknowledging the Thought Behind as well as the thing itself. Covetousness involves suspicion about the goodness and love of God, and even His justice. He has not given me what He gave somebody else. He doesn't notice my need. He doesn't love me as much as He loves him. He isn't fair.

Faith looks up with open hands. "You are giving me this, Lord? Thank You. It is good and acceptable and perfect."

The third lesson is that things can be *material for sacrifice*. This is what is called the eucharistic life. The Father pours out His blessings on us; we, His creatures, receive them with open hands, give thanks, and lift them up as an offering back to Him, thus completing the circle.

When Solomon's temple was about to be built, King David asked who was willing to give with open hands to the Lord. The people responded and gave gold, silver, bronze, iron, and precious stones. David then poured out his praise and thanksgivings:

Thine, O Lord, is the greatness, the power, the glory, the splendour, and the majesty; for everything in heaven and on earth is thine. . . . But what am I, and what is my people, that we should be able to give willingly like this? For everything comes from thee, and it is only of thy gifts that we give to thee.

The people joined in this praise, prostrating themselves before the Lord and the king, and the next day they celebrated with sacrifices of oxen, rams, lambs, and drink offerings, "with great rejoicing."

". . . There should be no reluctance, no sense of compulsion; God loves a cheerful giver. And it is in God's power to provide you richly with every good gift; thus you will have ample means in yourselves to meet each and every situation, with enough and to spare for every good cause."

It is said that Hudson Taylor, founder of the China Inland Mission, once a year sorted through everything he owned. Things that he had not used for a year were given away. He believed he would be held accountable for what he retained and there was no reason to retain things someone else could use as long as he himself had not needed them for a year's time.

Some of us are hoarders. Frugality is one thing, hoarding another. Having lived in a country where an ordinary mayonnaise jar was worth fifty cents without the mayonnaise makes me extremely careful about what I throw away. I believe in conserving as many plastic bags and wire twisters for closing them as I can readily use. My stinginess in the use of wax paper and paper towels amounts almost to an obsession. I have been known to dry out the paper towels used for blotting lettuce leaves—but I lived for eleven years in a place where there were no such things, so they are still luxuries to me.

I know one lady, however, who has cupboards full of cracked and chipped dishes, foil pans from frozen foods, plastic containers from cottage cheese and ice cream, and throwaway forks and spoons—quantities to last till the millennium. Most of us have some area of our lives that is cluttered and needs to be cleared to make space for useful things. Why do we cling to the unnecessary? Is it that our security lies in the accumulation of material goods? Is there a sense of satisfaction in opening a closet and seeing fifty-nine pairs of shoes, forty-two blouses or shirts? Can anyone reasonably make use of six different sets of dishes? (I am greatly indebted to a woman in my Bible class who, when she found out that some of the other women were planning to go together to buy me a set of ordinary crockery, remembered an unused set of Lenox china she had received for a wedding present. She gave it to me.)

> Instruct those who are rich in this world's goods not to be proud, and not to fix their hopes on so uncertain a thing as money, but upon God. . . . Tell them to do good and to grow rich in noble actions, to be ready to give away and to share, and so acquire a treasure which will form a good foundation for the future. Thus they will grasp the life that is life indeed.

This lesson leads naturally to the fourth, which is that things are given to us *to enjoy for a while.*

Nothing has done more damage to the Christian view of life than the hideous notion that those who are truly spiritual have lost all interest in this world and its beauties. The Bible says, ". . . God . . . endows us richly with all things to enjoy." It also says, "Do not set your hearts on the godless world or anything in it." It is altogether fitting and proper that we should enjoy things made for us to enjoy. What is not at all fitting or proper is that we should set our hearts on them. Temporal things must be treated as temporal things—received, given thanks for, offered back, but *enjoyed*. They must not be treated like eternal things.

Jesus said, "Beware! Be on your guard against greed of every kind, for even when a man has more than enough, his wealth does not give him life." He went on to tell the story of a man whose crops yielded so much that he had to pull down his barns to build bigger ones. Then he sat back and told himself confidently, ". . . Take life easy, eat, drink, and enjoy yourself.

"But God said to him, 'You fool, this very night you must surrender your life; you have made your money—who will get it now?' That is how it is with the man who amasses wealth for himself and remains a pauper in the sight of God."

"Do not store up for yourselves treasure on earth, where it grows rusty and moth-eaten, and thieves break in to steal it. Store up treasure in heaven, where there is no moth and no rust to spoil it, no thieves to break in and steal. For where your treasure is, there will your heart be also."

I must confess there was a sense of liberation when my silver was gone. I had felt uneasy each time we left the house. There had been a series of burglaries in our neighborhood, and we knew we were probably on the list. The police were fairly sure they knew who was doing it, but seemed powerless to do anything about it before or after. When it happened, I was shocked, but very quickly was able to say, "Well, so much for that. Thank You, Lord." My heart was lighter. We spent some of the insurance money on a set of plated silver that I suppose nobody is going to want very badly.

The young Francis of Assisi, believing that he was to be espoused to "Lady Poverty," stripped off his clothes and threw them on the ground.

"From now on," he said to the crowd in front of the

bishop's palace, "I can advance naked before the Lord, saying in truth no longer: my father, Peter Bernardone, but: our Father which art in Heaven!"

The bishop's gardener gave him a little coat, full of holes, on which he drew a chalk cross. Then he set out through the woods, singing the Lord's praises at the top of his lungs.

Not all Christians are bound to strip themselves naked and go singing into the woods, but all Christians are bound to have the same attitude of utter freedom from anxiety that enabled Saint Francis to sing.

The heart that is reluctant to receive joyfully all of God's good gifts is also reluctant to part with any of them.

A man who had great possessions came asking Jesus what he must do to gain eternal life. Jesus said he must keep the commandments. He had done so, the man said. What else was necessary?

"If you wish to go the whole way, sell your possessions . . . and come, follow me."

The man's attitude toward his possessions is revealed in his going away with a heavy heart. He could not know freedom as long as he clung to them. He came to Jesus with the burden of riches. He went away just as heavily laden when Jesus had wanted to give him rest.

Among my smaller possessions is one that seems a very great gift of civilization—an electric blanket. Here in New England, where our efforts to conserve fuel force us to keep the house a little cooler than an igloo, it is delicious to climb into a prewarmed bed. I am also thankful for clean sheets dried by sun and wind; for cream on my Grape-Nuts Flakes; for supermarkets and a car to get to them; for the telephone, electricity, and plumbing. I know very well they are all gifts, wholly undeserved, every one of them removable faster than it takes to list them and yet meant to be enjoyed if they are given.

116

"But aren't material things the enemy of the spiritual?" you ask.

The answer is no. It is a heresy ancient in origin but common in every age to imagine that there is a dichotomy between what is seen and what is unseen. The seen *proceeds from* the unseen.

"By faith we perceive that the universe was fashioned by the word of God, so that the visible came forth from the invisible."

Dualism holds that to escape, repress, or ignore the material is good. The body is in itself a prison from which the soul must escape. Christianity is not dualism. The body is not evil. Jesus Christ came down from heaven, was incarnate by the Holy Ghost, and was made man, thus forever sanctifying visible things. God is not looking for men and women who will learn to hate what He has made, but for those who will learn to love it as He loves it, as proceeding from Him and going back to Him.

"Will God take my possessions from me?" you ask.

If that is the only way He can get your attention, He may indeed. If loss will help to shift your perspective on the relative worth of things seen and unseen, He may indeed. The apostle Paul claimed to have suffered the loss of everything for Christ's sake. ". . . I count it so much garbage, for the sake of gaining Christ and finding myself incorporate in him. . . . All I care for is to know Christ. . . ."

The most overwhelming losses of my life, those that I feared most, have in fact been ". . . far outweighed by the gain of knowing Christ Jesus my Lord. . . ." I can never prove it to anybody. I cannot demonstrate it logically or scientifically. I only know that it is true and would say so with all my heart to others who, desiring to know Christ in all His fullness—in the power of His resurrection and in the fellowship of His suffering—yet fear loss. Do not be afraid.

Do not be afraid. Do not be afraid. The gain will outweigh everything.

"Yes, the troubles which are soon over, though they weigh little, train us for the carrying of a weight of eternal glory which is out of all proportion to them. . . . for visible things last only for a time, and the invisible things are eternal."

But still a fear remains.

"Suppose God does not actually take my possessions from me. Does He ask me to give them up?"

George MacDonald has some "carrion comfort" here:

> Are you so well satisfied with what you are, that you have never sought eternal life, never hungered and thirsted after the righteousness of God, the perfection of your being? If this latter be your condition, then be comforted; the Master does not require of you to sell what you have and give to the poor. *You* follow Him! *You* go with Him to preach good tidings!— you who care not for righteousness! You are not one whose company is desirable to the Master. Be comforted, I say: He does not want you; He will not ask you to open your purse for Him; you may give or withhold: it is nothing to Him. . . . *Go and keep the commandments.* It is not come to your money yet. The commandments are enough for you. You are not yet a child in the kingdom. You do not care for the arms of your Father; you value only the shelter of His roof. As to your money, let the commandments direct you how to use it. It is in you but pitiable presumption to wonder whether it is required of you to sell all that you have . . . for the Young Man to have sold all and followed Him would have been to accept God's patent of peerage: to you it is not offered.
>
> Does this comfort you? Then alas for you! . . . Your relief is to know that the Lord has no need of you—does not require you to part with your money, does not offer you Himself in-

stead. You do not indeed sell Him for thirty pieces of silver, but you are glad not to buy Him with all that you have.

"But," you say, "I do seek eternal life. I do most earnestly hunger and thirst for righteousness. I care for the Father's arms. Shall I then forsake everything I own, today, literally?"

I can only say this: God may ask it of you someday. If He does, I believe He will first prepare you for it and test the validity of your claim to willingness by smaller commitments.

Do you tithe? Money is a good place to begin, since it is the thing we are touchiest about. I know of one Southern Baptist church where every Sunday morning the congregation rises to their feet and says, "The Bible teaches it. I believe it. Tithe." The offering is then taken, averaging around $30,000 per week.

A tithe is a tenth. In Old Testament times the people of Israel gave a tenth of all they possessed—flocks, fruits, crops, money. Should we who live "under grace" do less than was required by law? We should let our offerings be a "first charge" to the Lord.

"Honour the Lord with your wealth as the first charge on all your earnings; then your granaries will be filled with corn and your vats bursting with new wine."

"Must I give a tenth of the gross or a tenth of after-tax income?" If you find it hard to do either, it is not likely that God is yet inviting you to forsake *all* to follow Him.

Another possible test: how do you respond when your possessions are damaged, destroyed, stolen?

Are you willing to be defrauded? Do you demand payment?

Are you upset by any infringement on your "right" to possess? Are you worried about what belongs to you? Are your fists clenched or are your palms open? Who is your master—God or money? What are you running after?

Clothes, food, money: "All these are things for the heathen to run after, not for you, because your heavenly Father knows that you need them all. Set your mind on God's kingdom and his justice before everything else, and all the rest will come to you as well. So do not be anxious about tomorrow; tomorrow will look after itself. . . ."

So we are back again to the first lesson. Things are given by God. We can trust Him to give to us. My little dog, Mac-Duff, taught me many lessons. How simple life was for him! He trusted me. He lived his life one day at a time, wearing his one ragged black coat, provided by a heavenly Father, appropriate to all occasions, all year round. Supper was there in the dish—Ken L Ration, Gainesburgers, table scraps, whatever. No decisions about the menu troubled him. He owned a house and a tremendous yard and quite a few squirrels and rabbits that he felt responsible to chase and bark at, but he had no taxes or mortgage payments. Everything was taken care of. What he did naturally is a hard lesson we human beings have to work at.

C. S. Lewis wrote to the American Lady, when she had a financial crisis, "I suppose living from day to day ('take no thought for the morrow') is precisely what we have to learn—though the Old Adam in me sometimes murmurs that if God wanted me to live like the lilies of the field, I wonder He didn't give me the same lack of nerves and imagination they enjoy!"

Four lessons, then:

1. Things are given by God
2. Things are to be received with thanksgiving
3. Things are material for sacrifice
4. Things are given us to enjoy for a while

And there is a fifth: all that belongs to Christ is ours, therefore, as Amy Carmichael wrote, "All that was ever ours is ours forever."

We often say that what is ours belongs to Christ. Do we remember the opposite: that what is His is ours? That seems to me a wonderful truth, almost an incredible truth. If it is so, how can we really "lose" anything? How can we even speak of His having the "right" to *our* possessions?

"Everything belongs to you! Paul, Apollos or Cephas; the world, life, death, the present or the future, everything is yours! For you belong to Christ, and Christ belongs to God!"

"Son, thou art ever with me, and all that I have is thine," the Father says to us. That is riches.

TWELVE

The Discipline of Work

THERE IS NO SUCH THING as Christian work. That is, there is no work in the world which is, in and of itself, Christian. Christian work is any kind of work, from cleaning a sewer to preaching a sermon, that is done by a Christian and offered to God.

This means that nobody is excluded from serving God. It means that no work is "beneath" a Christian. It means there is no job in the world that needs to be boring or useless. A Christian finds fulfillment not in the particular kind of work he does, but in the way in which he does it. Work done for Christ all the time must be "full-time Christian work."

Tax gatherers and soldiers were among those who came out into the wilderness to be baptized by John. When they asked what they ought to do to prove their repentance, John did not tell them to give up their jobs and start doing what he did. To tax gatherers he said, "Exact no more than the assessment." To the soldiers, ". . . No bullying; no blackmail; make do with your pay!" This way of doing their particular jobs would certainly be a radically new direction. A tax collector who took no more than was legally required or a soldier who never bullied, never blackmailed, never protested for higher pay would be a nonconformist of the first water.

Every one of us has a line of duty marked out for us by God. For most human beings, for most of history, there has been little choice available. We tend to forget this in a time when the options seem limitless and when "what one does" usually means specifically his money-earning capacities. Duty, however, includes whatever we ought to do for others—make a bed, give someone a ride to church, mow a lawn, clean a garage, paint a house. It is often possible to "get out of" work like that. Nobody is paying us. It simply needs to be done, and if we don't do it, nobody will. But the nature of the work changes when we see that it is God who marks out this line of duty for us. It is service to Him. When we see Him, we may say, "Lord, when did I ever mow *Your* lawn? When did I iron *Your* clothes?" He will answer, "When you did it for one of the least of my children, you did it for me."

Brother Lawrence practiced the presence of God in the kitchen of a monastery. Sophie the Scrubwoman did floors for Jesus. Dag Hammarskjöld as secretary general of the United Nations offered his work to God, finding the explanation of how a man should live a life of active social service in the writings of the great medieval mystics:

> For whom "self-surrender" had been the way to self-realization, and who in "singleness of mind" and "inwardness" had found strength to say Yes to every demand which the needs of their neighbors made them face, and to say Yes also to every fate life had in store for them. . . . Love—that much misused and misinterpreted word—for them meant simply an overflowing of the strength with which they felt themselves filled when living in true self-oblivion. And this love found natural expression in an unhesitant fulfillment of duty and an unreserved acceptance of life, whatever it brought them personally of toil, suffering—or happiness.

A diary entry in 1956 reads:

Before Thee, Father
In righteousness and humility,

With Thee, Brother,
In faith and courage,

In Thee, Spirit,
In stillness.

Thine, for Thy will is my destiny,
Dedicated—for my destiny is to be used and used up according
   to Thy will.

What are the demands that the needs of our families or
neighbors lay upon us? That is the line of duty God has
marked out for us. It was plain enough to me, when I was a
close observer of the life of jungle Indians, that they all did
what they had to do to survive, from the smallest child who
could walk to the old grandmother who still took her basket
and went out to plant manioc in the family clearing. There
were few choices indeed. They did not congratulate themselves on doing their duty. It certainly never entered their
heads that they were virtuous for doing it. Duty is *good.*
When we do it, we are doing good, but are not thereby gaining merit.

It is wrong to draw so many distinctions between what we
can't "get out of" doing—that is, what is necessary for sur-
vival—and what we choose to do. The eight-hour-daily job
for which we are being paid is a duty as well as a physical
necessity. Many of the things we do "after work," unless we
are demoniacally selfish people, are work, too, often for
others. Are they so different in God's eyes? I doubt it. The
work assigned to me includes writing and speaking, forms of
service often labeled "full-time Christian," but my service to
God also includes housework and correspondence and being
available to help family and friends do things that need

doing. If my husband needs a haircut or a letter typed, I'm available.

"We shall not make any wild claims," Paul wrote to the Corinthians, "but simply judge ourselves by that line of duty which God has marked out for us, and that line includes our work on your behalf. We do not exceed our duty when we embrace your interests, for it was our preaching of the gospel which brought us into contact with you. Our pride is not in matters beyond our proper sphere, nor in the labours of other men."

What is our "proper sphere"? We cannot dismiss the fact of modern life: there are indeed many choices when it comes to discerning that sphere. Let us rest assured that God knows how to show His will to one who is willing to do it. The place to begin discovering the larger sphere is in the smaller one— in the willingness to say yes to every demand that the need of a neighbor makes us face.

A young couple came to ask my advice about the wife's work. The man was in school, so it was necessary for her to work to pay the bills. This is one of the hard realities today and puts a strain on any marriage. I believe it can be a workable arrangement as long as it is seen, by both parties, as a temporary expedient until such time as it is possible for the husband to assume the responsibility laid upon hus-bands—to cherish their wives, to make it possible for them to have a family, and then to provide for it. This was not the major difficulty of the young couple. Both saw the situation as temporary, not ideal. The problem was that she was not finding her work very "fulfilling." Should she take the risk of quitting a boring job and just hope that the Lord would lead her to a better one? Of course it was a question I could not answer for them, but I tried to help them see the whole thing in a different light.

First, her working was an economic necessity since he

could not work. Any job was better than no job. Second, it was temporary. She need not think of it as a career. She wanted to be a mother. Third—and they had not thought of this—"fulfillment" is not to be found in any job in the world, *as a job*. She was mistaken to be looking for fulfillment there. The job was "beneath" her, she felt—she was "over-qualified," having a degree that had nothing to do with that type of work and was therefore going to waste. Was she willing to do anything that their present need required—for her husband's sake—as unto the Lord? Was she willing to forego all thought of personal satisfaction in the job and aim instead at satisfying the Master? (How could I convince her that the satisfaction of doing a job for Him would be infinitely greater than the rewards using her so-called qualifications might bring?)

I don't know what happened to them. Perhaps God provided an interesting and challenging position for her. If not, I hope they learned the essential lesson: interest and challenge can always be found in any task done for God. If our work seems to be beneath us, if it becomes boring and meaningless, mere drudgery, it may be a living, but it is not living. It is not the life of freedom and fullness a disciple's life is designed to be.

Does God ask us to do what is beneath us? This question will never trouble us again if we consider the Lord of heaven taking a towel and washing feet.

In the time of the church's beginnings when the Twelve needed someone to look after the daily distribution to widows, they said it would be a grave mistake for them to neglect the Word of God to "serve tables." That they did not mean the job was beneath them is clear from the kind of men they sought to fill the position: ". . . men of good reputation . . . full of the Spirit and of wisdom. . . ." The apostles themselves, remember, were untrained laymen to begin with, but they had been clearly called to the ministry of the Word. Different men have different gifts, different responsibilities, and even serving tables requires the Spirit and wisdom. Both kinds of work needed to be done in the church, and they looked to the Lord for His appointments. It is especially interesting that one of the men appointed was Stephen, "full of grace and power," whose acceptance of responsibility for the Greek widows soon led to his doing great miracles and signs (who knows whether he was the first to conciliate them, and this in itself was seen to be a miracle?) and to his speaking with such inspired wisdom that he excited the extreme jealousy and irrational hatred of the religious elite. He must have been a truly humble man to have accepted that first task and a very brilliant man to have made such an impression as a speaker. God prepared him for martyrdom by giving him a mundane job.

A good many foolish notions about what makes a great martyr would dissolve if we traced the story of the church's first one.

Chapter 1: A dispute between Greeks and Jews about the widows' dole

Chapter 2: Stephen appointed to a committee to wait tables

Chapter 3: He begins working miracles

Chapter 4: Called on the carpet by the Synagogue of Freedmen

Chapter 5: Stephen's defense and vision of the Son of Man

Chapter 6: Stoned to death

What constitutes a "great work for God"? Where does it begin? Always in humility. Not in being served, but in serving. Not in self-actualization but in self-surrender.

I once heard a formula guaranteed to prevent boredom: it is to have

1. Something to do
2. Someone to love
3. Something to look forward to

The Christian has all these in Christ: work, a Master, a hope. Yet how easily we forget this. One of the results of the Fall is that we lose sight of the meaning of things and begin to see the world as dull and opaque, instead of charged with glory. What other people are doing looks much more interesting and exciting than what we have to do. There is no "magic" in *my* routine, we think—but hers looks enviable.

If Stephen had set his heart on the working of miracles and signs or on becoming a brilliant apologist, he would hardly have been willing to accept an appointment on the welfare board. That, however, was what happened to be open to him at the moment. There was a need. He was called upon to fill it. He said yes. His heart was set on one thing: obedience to God. He was counted worthy to suffer because he was willing to serve. Stephen did not lift up his soul unto vanity, dreaming of attaining a place of high distinction in church history.

"Who shall ascend into the hill of the Lord, or who shall stand in his holy place? He that hath clean hands and a pure heart. . . ."

Let us lift up our work as we lift up our hands, our hearts, our bodies—a sacrifice, acceptable because it is lifted up to Him who alone can purify. Without this offering, the thing dies. Deadness, lifelessness, boredom are inevitable.

Even the work of writing ("Christian" books!) can become dull. It looks wonderfully exciting to many. I know, because they come to me with eyes shining and speak of how wonderful it must be.

"I'm hoping to write a book someday," they say, "when I have time ... when the children are grown ... when I retire."

I encourage them to do it, by all means. But if they ask if I love to write, is it pure pleasure, do I ever find it hard, I must admit that for me the process is always hard. I must make myself tackle it, day after day.

Yesterday, for example, was bad. I had the whole day to myself, in a quiet place. There was not the slightest chance, barring some dire emergency, of any interruptions. I knew what I had to do. I had notes prepared. I had the typewriter, the paper, the place to work. I am in excellent health. The temperature was perfect—not too hot, not too cold. If you can't work under conditions like these, you can't work at all. I kept telling myself this.

But I did not feel like working. That's what it came down to. I was restless, distracted, and disgusted with myself. I wondered if I had "shot my bolt," as the English say. Maybe I really had nothing to say after all. It had all been said, of course, and maybe it had all been said by me. I was repeating myself. Alas. Furthermore, if it hadn't been said, what did I know about it anyway? The thoughts that there were probably still some readers out there somewhere who would like what I wrote and that I had just had another letter from a kind publisher expressing interest in what I might write next did not really help. ". . . Of making many books there is no end, and much study is a weariness of the flesh" was the only verse that spoke loud and clear to me. I thought of all those Christian bookstores, filled with the avalanche of bright paperbacks that pour daily off the presses; of the full-color brochures and full-page advertisements for the newest blockbuster. I remembered some depressing statistics I had read: by age sixteen, most children have spent 10,000–15,000 hours watching television. Seventy-four percent of adult Americans don't read a single book from one year to the next. We're the "nonreadingest" country in the industrialized world.

I pictured the gigantic booksellers' convention I will be attending in a few weeks. Alas again. Why add yet another book to the pile?

The job that surely is one of the world's pleasantest does not always hold much appeal to the one whose job it happens to be. This is the very point we need to get hold of—the enemy has plenty of means of dulling the shine, distracting us, making us bored with whatever is given us to do, making it appear worthless. It is difficult to keep in mind the spiritual character of our work (for there is spiritual character to all work that God gives us). It requires spiritual protection. "Organizations and powers that are spiritual" are against us, to drag us down to discouragement, disgust, despair.

"And let the beauty of the Lord our God be upon us: and establish thou the work of our hands ..." must be our prayer. We need help. We may write the book, sell the policy, cook the meal, do the job, whatever it is, but there will be days when we do it halfheartedly, other days when we do it despondently. If the work is soaked in prayer, the beauty will be there, the work will be established.

Work is a blessing. God has so arranged the world that work is necessary, and He gives us hands and strength to do it. The enjoyment of leisure would be nothing if we had only leisure. It is the joy of work well done that enables us to enjoy rest, just as it is the experiences of hunger and thirst that make food and drink such pleasures.

I never appreciated the tremendous therapeutic value of

work until I lost my first husband. Since then I have been asked dozens of times, "How did you ever bring yourself to go back to the jungle?"

I doubt that I could have. I did not "go back." I stayed. There was work to be done, lots of work, and there was nobody else to do it. Every day, from the first day following the final news that five men were dead, was packed with duties. My baby, my house, an airstrip to maintain, Indians to teach and employ and visit and inject and advise and help, translation work and correspondence filled the time I might otherwise have used to feel sorry for myself.

My second husband's death, a long and agonizing process, made me unutterably grateful to God for plain, ordinary housework. It was just cooking for him—and racking my brains to come up with menus he would be able to enjoy at least a little bit—and cleaning and washing his dishes and clothes and sheets, carrying trays, keeping track of his medicines and answering his letters that got me through. I would find myself thanking God for a pile of dishes or laundry.

It is the one for whom a job is done who gives it its meaning. Of course I was not thinking about frying pans or laundry detergents when I was frying an egg or washing. I was thinking of Add. As the disease progressed, however, he became extremely depressed and no longer wanted to eat, to be read to, bathed, dressed, or cared for in any way. I was like the "troubler of Israel" to him, and he told me so. Nevertheless the work still had to be done. Even when he was at his worst and I was barely able to get through a day, the work was there, and by the grace of God I did it. When I remembered to look up instead of around me and to offer the work to the Lord, it was much easier and more pleasant.

There are many people who have no one on earth to do their work *for*. The boss is a hard woman to be avoided at all costs; there is no family at home waiting for the paycheck; nobody really cares whether they like their jobs; nobody thanks them. What does the discipline of work mean for them?

What Paul had to say to the slaves in the church in Colossae should help us here. "Slaves, give entire obedience to your earthly masters, not merely with an outward show of service, to curry favour with men, but with single-mindedness, out of reverence for the Lord. Whatever you are doing, put your whole heart into it, as if you were doing it for the Lord and not for men, knowing that there is a Master who will give you your heritage as a reward for your service. Christ is the Master whose slaves you must be."

I try to imagine what it would be like to be a slave during the time of the Roman Empire. We who live in a free country in this century bring to our imaginings many factors that probably did not trouble them then. Few, I suppose, gave much thought to the moral question of slavery. Many were glad to have somebody else in charge of their lives, as many today are glad, even though they would not want the label of slaves. I feel fairly sure, however, that giving *entire obedience* to an earthly master was not easier for first-century slaves than it is for twentieth-century employees and/or disciples. It was undoubtedly a good deal harder. Working with single-mindedness, out of reverence for the Lord, has always been difficult if for no other reason than that the enemy of our souls would rather we be double-minded and see only the human boss, with all his failings. If there was a slave driver cracking a whip for fourteen hours a day, imagine putting your whole heart into it.

The Christian attitude toward work is truly revolutionary. Think what it would do to the economy and the entire fabric of life if the question were asked daily, in the kitchen, in the office, the schoolroom, the plant: "Who is your Master?" and the answer were given: "Christ is my Master, whose slave I am." It would transform in a stroke not only the worker's attitude toward the boss, but his attitude toward those who work with him. No longer would he be scheming ways to outdo them, cheat them, gain preference over them in the employer's eyes. He would not be seeking ways to evade work that he doesn't like and letting George do it. It would change his attitude toward the work itself because he would do it not for show, not for promotion or bonuses or compliments or the free trip to Las Vegas, but with single-mindedness, for Christ. It would change the quality of the work, for he has a master who sees what no other overseer could spot: not only every detail of the work done, but the intentions of the heart. The workman would know that the work, no matter how demeaning it might otherwise be, how routine, how humble, really does matter. It will be noticed.

When Lars and I climbed the tower of Norwich cathedral, we discovered, far up in the narrowest, darkest stairway, a few small faces carved into the stone. Who was the workman who chiseled them? For whom? Did he expect the public to acknowledge his work in so obscure a place? He must have done it for God.

Think of the brightness there will be in the place where work is done for God. Think of the peace in the heart of the workman who lifts it up to Him.

Not only is work itself a blessing. The ability to work is a gift. Ask Joni Eareckson. She is paralyzed. She can no longer do the normal work given to the rest of us, but she has learned, through excruciating practice and discipline, to do things in extraordinary ways. She paints, holding the brush in her mouth. She drives a van specially adapted for her needs. She writes books, travels, speaks, works for the handicapped. To see her do these things against such terrific odds makes me aware of blessings I took for granted. My legs carry me where I want to go, my hands hold a vacuum cleaner, my fingers work—all ten of them—to fix my hair, knead bread, play the piano, type.

Each separate ability is a gift. Moses was a great man, greatly gifted, chosen to lead the people of Israel out of bondage, shown the pattern of the tabernacle on Mount Sinai: make Me a sanctuary. Make an ark. Make a table. Make a lampstand. Make the hangings. Make a veil.

Who would carry out the intricate instructions?

"Mark this," Moses said to the Israelites, "the Lord has specially chosen Bezalel son of Uri, son of Hur, of the tribe of Judah. He has filled him with divine spirit, making him skilful and ingenious, expert in every craft, and master of design, whether in gold, silver, and copper, or cutting precious stones for setting, or carving wood, in every kind of design. He has inspired both him and Aholiab . . . to instruct workers and designers of every kind, engravers, seamsters, embroiderers in violet, purple, and scarlet yarn and fine linen, and weavers, fully endowing them with skill to execute all kinds of work. Bezalel and Aholiab shall work exactly as the Lord has commanded. . . ."

Saint Benedict's Rule for Monasteries states that the first degree of humility is obedience without delay.

> But this very obedience will be acceptable to God and pleasing to men only if what is commanded is done without hesitation, delay, lukewarmness, grumbling, or objection. For the obedience given to superiors is given to God, since He Himself has said, "He who hears you, hears Me." And the disciples should offer their obedience with a good will, for "God loves a cheerful giver." For if the disciple obeys with an

ill will and murmurs, not necessarily with his lips but simply in his heart, then even though he fulfills the command yet his work will not be acceptable to God, who sees that his heart is murmuring.

Father Jude, of Saint Gregory's Priory, writes:

The table blessing at our noon meal on Sundays is different from the everyday one. The two monks who have been serving tables during the week just ended begin it by saying together a verse from Psalm 86, "Blessed are you, O Lord God, for you have helped and strengthened me." . . . I find it a solemn and affecting moment. It typifies the kind of life we give ourselves to, one which invests ordinary, everyday actions with spiritual significance. It is a comfort to know that when we minister to the needs of others, even if the ministry is only the fetching of food for them to eat and taking away their used dishes, we are appropriating the grace of God in doing it. . . .

It is a legitimately enjoyable luxury to come to lunch or supper, sit down and eat, and leave without having to do anything more about it. In due course, the time will come when it is your turn to be the servant . . . but this need not make present repose less enjoyable. It is useful to learn to take one's proper ease, both in body and spirit.

Are not the psalm verses at the Sunday blessing a bit overwrought? ("O God, make speed to save me, O Lord, make haste to help me!" It sounds like a perilous undertaking. "Blessed are you, O Lord God, for you have helped and strengthened me!" We made it! We got through it!) Perhaps not, though, if we remember that we minister with the power of God Himself. To undertake ministry at whatever level is an audacious step. One hardly ever needs humility more than when he is being useful. . . . The body that I am helping to keep alive is destined for a glorious resurrection. The person to whom I am carrying a plate of food is someone whom it is an honor to serve. For he has been invited to eat and drink at the table of a King.

A Christian is characterized by a willingness to work. Laziness was so serious an offense that Paul told the Thessalonians to hold aloof from anyone who fell into idle habits. He himself had never accepted board or lodging from anyone without paying for it.

> We toiled and drudged, we worked for a living night and day, rather than be a burden to any of you. . . . we laid down the rule: the man who will not work shall not eat. We mention this because we hear that some of your number are idling their time away, minding everybody's business but their own. To all such we give these orders, and we appeal to them in the name of the Lord Jesus Christ to work quietly for their living.

Not long ago a young woman asked me to pray that she would find a job. As we talked, I learned that she badly wanted to get into radio and television work, but so far had not found anything in that field. She had been on unemployment compensation for two years. I suggested that she could probably find work cleaning. She was shocked and offended. "But I have a master's degree!"

"The man who will not work shall not eat." It was Paul's word, not mine, and I presume it would apply to a woman who has no one to feed her but the federal government. The young woman's case was not one of inability to work because of poor health or the care of small children. She simply was unwilling to work—unless she liked the job. Let us never say, "God has given me nothing to do." He has. It lies on your doorstep. Do it, and He will show you something else.

"We want you not to become lazy, but to imitate those who, through faith and patience, are inheriting the promises."

When I was in the sixth grade, one of our penmanship exercises was this verse, which has rung in my mind ever since:

> If a task is once begun
> Never leave it till it's done.
> Be the labor great or small,
> Do it well or not at all.

We will finish our course with joy if we stick to the assignment. We will be able to say as Jesus did, "I have finished the work You gave me."

THIRTEEN

The Discipline of Feelings

"I HAVE A LOT of trouble with this," said the student. "I mean, I'm just not sure how to work this out comfortably."

"Work it out comfortably?" queried the Bible teacher. "What has that got to do with the will of God?"

The phraseology may be new ("feeling comfortable" has become terribly important) but there is nothing new about the reluctance. Jesus made it vivid in His parable of the man who gave a big dinner party. When the invitations went out, the excuses began to come in: "I have bought some land." "I am on my way to try out my new yoke of oxen." "I just got married." Unable to work things out comfortably, they declined the invitation.

Feelings, like thoughts, must be brought into captivity. No one whose first concern is feeling good can be a disciple. We are called to carry a cross and to glorify God. P. T. Forsyth notes that the weakness of much popular religion is due to having gotten one of the basic tenets of our faith backwards, making it "God's chief end is to glorify man." People are acted on by suggestion rather than authority. Years ago Seven Oxford Men wrote a book called *Foundations*, which was an attempt to allow all Christians to believe what they liked. Ronald Knox said, "They corrected 'I believe' to 'one does feel.' "

The story of Daniel provides a strong lesson in the victory of a God-directed will over the natural emotions. Daniel was given vision, insight, and prophecy, but his understanding came at tremendous cost. He had to be humbled. The process began, as we noted earlier, by his own resolve not to defile himself with the king's rich diet. A resolve is not a mood. The word does not describe the effects of circumstances on the psyche. It has nothing to do with feeling comfortable. It is a decision of the will, carried out without regard to the emotions. In fasting, according to a sixth-century Latin hymn, "Daniel trained his mystic sight."

Because of superior performance of duty, Daniel was the object of great hatred and envy. His rivals hatched a plot to have him put to death. We can guess at Daniel's feelings as he sensed their hatred, faced the possible consequences, made the life-and-death decision to continue his prayers to his God ("do not wait for desire before performing a virtuous deed, since reason and understanding are sufficient," wrote Saint John of the Cross), was apprehended, brought before the king, and sentenced. Imagine that night with the lions. Imagine hearing the voice of the terrified king as he came, trembling, to the pit the next morning and called out, "Daniel, servant of the living God, has your God whom you serve continually been able to save you from the lions?"

". . . No trace of injury was found on him, because he had put his faith in his God."

Daniel paid a high price for the divine revelations he was given. It was no emotional high that he experienced. In fact, he wrote that his spirit within him was ". . . troubled, and, dismayed . . ." by the vision; ". . . my thoughts dismayed me greatly and I turned pale . . ."; ". . . I was trying to understand. . . . I was seized with terror. . . . my strength failed me and I lay sick for a while. . . ." But, "Then I rose and attended to the king's business. . . ."

"Troubled soul, thou art not bound to feel, but thou art bound to arise," wrote George MacDonald.

The account goes on. When a prophecy concerning the kings of Persia was given to him:

> ... It cost him much toil to understand it.... "I was left alone ... my strength left me; I became a sorry figure of a man and retained no strength.... I fell prone on the ground in a trance. Suddenly a hand grasped me and pulled me up on to my hands and knees. He said to me, 'Daniel, man greatly beloved, attend to the words I am speaking to you and stand up where you are, for I am now sent to you.' ... I stood up trembling.... I hung my head and was struck dumb."

He opened his mouth to speak; strength failed him; no breath was left in him.

"Do not be afraid, man greatly beloved; all will be well with you. Be strong, be strong," was the angel's word to him.

Is there a more vivid and powerful picture in all of Scripture of a man, thoroughly human, racked with passions and fears, a man of deep and disturbing emotions who yet held faithfully to his God and acted for Him in spite of natural inclination? Only the picture of Christ Himself, the perfect servant, surpasses that of Daniel. It is clear in Daniel's story that understanding is not cheap and that answers to prayer must be processed, often over a long period of time, requiring steadfast endurance. It is worth pausing a moment to ponder what the angel said. It was not, "I know how you feel," or, "You've really had it tough, old boy," but, "Do not be afraid. Be strong." The angel reminded him of two things that are true of the rest of us: he was greatly loved, and all would be well. Next time our feelings seem about to drown us, we may think on those things and be strong.

My friend Katherine Morgan, of Pasto, Colombia, wrote:

When one thinks and uses the arm of faith to back one's thinking, then the works of faith are produced. I agree with you that feelings are untrustworthy. Human thinking is also untrustworthy, but faith which wings our thoughts heavenward is productive, such as Ezekiel's experience when God told him his wife would die. He did as he was commanded. I think you and I had this experience. Our feelings were conducive to doubt as to the reasons why our husbands were taken, but we knew inside we had to do as the Lord had commanded. In my estimation there was no particular virtue in what we did. We had received our orders, and we had to stick by them and carry our feelings in our pockets. Many times my feelings would have led me to throw in the sponge here in Pasto. I "felt" the people were unresponsive and dull of hearing and the effort was fruitless. I "felt" everything but the desire to stay here and work. Nevertheless God's plan has to be carried out. This is a hard lesson to learn, and it often takes a lifetime. But one must have the conviction that God has spoken and then one must get busy and carry out the command.

I have seen how Katherine does that. Her house is a haven for an astonishing variety of people. There is never a time when she is not giving shelter and help and food and care and counsel and attention and money and clothing and whatever else is needed to the sick, the insane, the poor, even the criminal. They beat a path to her door. Everybody in Pasto knows the Señora Catalina. Anyone who does not know where else to turn turns to her.

"Mission" has always meant, at least in the Christian connotations of that term, not only the effort to convert someone to true faith, but also the spiritual disposition of the missionary: his active charity and his self-giving to the "object" of his missionary task. From St. Paul to St. Nicholas of Japan there has been no mission without self-identification of the missionary with those to whom God has sent him, without a sacrifice of his personal attachments and his natural values.

I am sure that Katherine Morgan values privacy and quietness as much as I do. They are among the many things she has blithely given up. I say blithely because she never talks about it as a sacrifice, never makes anything of it, does it quite as a matter of course, day in and day out, year after strenuous year. She doesn't bother to consult her feelings in the matter.

The people who do real work for God are nevertheless people with real feelings. On one occasion during the rebuilding of the wall of Jerusalem, the common people raised a great fuss against their fellow Jews about their methods of raising money to buy food and pay taxes. "I was very angry when I heard their outcry and the story they told," Nehemiah said. "I mastered my feelings and reasoned with the nobles and magistrates. I said, . . . 'What you are doing is wrong.' " Note that mastering his feelings did not mean smiling sweetly and saying "Everything's fine. You're okay."

The people had indeed done wrong to take persons as pledges for debts, and Nehemiah's anger was warranted. But the heat generated would contribute nothing to their edification. It had to be cooled before he could reason with the nobles and magistrates. He saw clearly what the issue was, in spite of arguments in favor of the practice, and declared it to be wrong.

The modern mind easily confuses emotions and facts. If it feels good, do it! What is good, it is generally assumed, ought to make us feel good. For example, if it is the will of God, we will feel good about it. This is not always the case. Jonah had no good feelings about going to Ninevah. He preferred Joppa and started in that direction, to his own sorrow and that of his shipmates.

The apostle Paul, who seems to many of us the man in the Bible most in control of his feelings, had to remind the crowd that he still had feelings. It was at Lystra, when he had commanded a cripple to stand straight up on his feet, and the man did so. This convinced the crowds that the gods had come down in human form. They named Paul and Barnabas Mercury and Jupiter and were prepared to offer sacrifice to them. "... What is this that you are doing?" shouted the apostle. "We are only human beings [men of like passions] no less mortal than you."

Elijah was a man with feelings, like the rest of us, yet when he prayed earnestly that it would not rain, "... not a drop fell on the land for three years and a half."

There is nothing in the Bible to suggest that truly holy people are those without feelings. The very opposite is true. Jesus was fully man and fully subject to the temptations of men. He showed deep and tender feelings (taking babies into his arms, weeping for Jerusalem and for His friend Lazarus), powerful anger (when He turned the money changers' tables upside down and drove them out of the temple with a whip), and before His actual physical suffering at the time of the crucifixion, He was in anguish of soul both at the supper table and later in Gethsemane. Yet He pursued His course. His face was set "like flint" to do the will of His Father, and no human feelings, overwhelming as they must have been, deterred Him.

Thomas Merton wrote that in Jesus we see "a supreme harmony between well-ordered human feelings and the demands of a divine nature and personality."

Are we to be mere victims of our feelings, like boats adrift without sail or rudder or anchor? Are we really at their mercy? If it feels good, we do it; if it doesn't, we don't—is that how the disciple is meant to live? Is that discipline?

The letter of Jude speaks of people who live by their feelings. Jude encourages the true Christians to put up a real fight against what these people, who have surreptitiously entered the church, stand for. "They have no real reverence for God, and they abuse His grace as an opportunity for immorality. They will not recognize the only Master, Jesus Christ our Lord."

The letter paints a picture of people who live by fantasy and appetite, showing contempt for authority and ready to mock at anything that doesn't come naturally. They live by instinct, like unreasoning beasts, like clouds driven by a wind, trees without fruit, raging waves of the sea, producing only "the spume of their own shameful deeds," like stars that follow no orbit, always trying to mold life by their own desires. They are led by emotion and never by the Spirit of God.

This points up the diametrical contrast between the two kingdoms: the one where my will is done and the one where God's will is done. The one that is darkness, the other that is light. And it points to a choice. If I insist on molding my life according to my own desire, so that I can always feel comfortable, I am by that insistence denying the Lord. I am not recognizing the only Master, Jesus Christ my Lord.

Paul spells out exactly what the lower nature is. It is all that is *against* God. "For the outlook of the lower nature is enmity with God...." "That nature sets its desires against the Spirit...." It is characterized by such things as fornication, impurity, and indecency, idolatry and sorcery, quarrels, a contentious temper, envy, fits of rage, selfish ambitions, dissensions, party intrigues, and jealousies. We may self-righteously claim that we are certainly not guilty of the first three, until we remember Jesus' words that if anyone even so much as *looks* lustfully, he has already committed adultery in his heart. We may dismiss the next two in the list, until we remember Samuel's word:

> Defiance of him [the Lord] is sinful as witchcraft,
> yielding to men as evil as idolatry.

Most of us will admit that there is no question that we are guilty of the rest of the sins in the list. Feelings play a strong part in every one of them. ". . . We were slaves to passions and pleasures of every kind, . . ." is Paul's description of how we all used to be.

What are we to do? Shall we accept the current idea that we should "go with our feelings," and if we don't we're not being "honest"?

How many divorces are "justified" on this ground? How many nasty remarks?

As with all other questions, let us take it to Scripture. We have no other norm. If there is a word spoken, we must hear and do it.

"So then, my brothers, you can see that we have no particular reason to feel grateful to our instinctive nature, or to live life on the level of the instincts. Indeed that way of living leads to certain spiritual death. . . ."

The world says, "Go with your feelings and be honest."

The Bible says, "Go with your feelings and die."

The world says, "Deny your feelings and you're dead."

The Bible says, "But if on the other hand you cut the nerve of your instinctive actions by obeying the Spirit, you are on the way to real living."

"You must not let yourselves be distressed," said Jesus to His disciples when He was about to leave them. It would surely be most natural to feel deep distress about His going away. "Don't allow yourselves to give way," He told them.

". . . Delight yourselves in the Lord! . . . a great safeguard to your souls," wrote Paul from his prison chains.

". . . If you are helping others in distress, do it cheerfully."

Of Hezekiah, who became king of Judah at the age of twenty-five, it is said that he *put* his trust in the Lord. That sounds quite deliberate. As a result of that choice, there was nobody like him among all the kings of Judah; he remained loyal to the Lord; he did not fail in his allegiance to Him; he kept the commandments, "So the Lord was with him and he prospered in all that he undertook. . . ." If there had been any reporter around to thrust a microphone in his face and ask how he felt about his role, I doubt that Hezekiah would have had a ready answer. His concern lay elsewhere.

Mozart, in contrast to many modern musicians, never used music to speak about himself, his situation, or his mood. In 1781 he wrote, "The emotions, strong or not, should never be expressed *ad nauseam,* and music must never offend the ears but must please them."

What sort of things will characterize the life of one who obeys the Spirit? ". . . Love, joy, peace, patience, kindness, goodness, fidelity, gentleness, and self-control."

Note that *self*-control is one of the fruits of the Spirit. Here is evidence again of man's responsibility to cooperate with God in His work. It is not all "Spirit control." Self-control is essential. The man who has accepted the rule of the Spirit in his life will accept spiritual discipline. In accepting the discipline of his Master, he will willingly discipline himself. This is a sign of spiritual maturity, just as it is a sign of emotional maturity. Both parent and child must suffer in the process of

146

child training, because punishment sometimes becomes a necessary part of that process. Therefore it is a great joy and a great release when the parent sees the child at last accepting responsibility and disciplining himself. He is beginning to mature. Our Father in heaven must be glad when His child learns to control himself and not to have to be held in with bit and bridle.

It is the will that must deal with the feelings. The will must triumph over them, but only the will that is surrendered to Christ can do this.

A young woman approached me following a talk I had given on the discipline of feeling. She was very puzzled.

"Mrs. Elliot, you look like you've really got it together. I mean, you're strong and everything, you know? But you must have had some really deep feelings sometime, didn't you? What I don't understand is, how did you get rid of them?"

Woe is me. Had I failed to explain that I was not talking about *getting rid* of feelings? Did she think I had reached some high spiritual plane where only the mind and spirit operated and feelings were extinct? I went over it again: as long as we live in the "body of this death" we shall struggle against the lower nature, against that which is always at war with God. The "evil that I would not" is still there. Feelings are strong, whether good ones or bad ones. Sometimes they help, sometimes they hinder. It is *discipline* we are discussing. If we are talking about disciplining a racehorse or a child, we are not talking about getting rid of either, but rather bringing them under control.

Choices will continually be necessary and—let us not forget—*possible*. Obedience to God is always possible. It is a deadly error to fall into the notion that when feelings are extremely strong we can do nothing but act on them.

It was the will of Jesus that triumphed in Gethsemane and then on the cross. We see evidence of the nearly overpowering feelings He experienced as a human being when His sweat fell like great drops of blood and He cried out, "If it be possible let this cup pass," and later when He was thirsty on the cross, and finally when He gave a great cry. The strength of His will is proved in His willing against Himself, that is, in His prayer "not my will but thine be done." There was a tremendous battle being waged between His natural human response to what was happening and His absolute desire to do the will of the Father. He had come to earth expressly to do that will. His purpose was simple. Carrying it out, however, was not easy. He could not possibly "feel comfortable" with it. But He did it. That is what matters. He did it. He was ". . . given up to death for our misdeeds. . . ."

It is a great temptation to look to special spiritual experiences as the test of holiness. To feel oneself carried away by the Spirit, to exhibit certain unusual manifestations, or to be thrilled by sudden exaltation in prayer or success in some particular effort made for God are all too often taken as proof positive that we are, at last, on the right wavelength.

Hannah Whitall Smith, in her book *Religious Fanaticism*, writes: "A quiet steadfast holding of the human will to the will of God and a peaceful resting in His love and care is of infinitely greater value in the religious life than the most intense emotions or the most wonderful experiences that have ever been known by the greatest mystic of them all."

Those who insist on such signs invariably split communities and draw attention to themselves rather than to Christ. It is Christ who is to be exalted, not our feelings. We will know Him by obedience, not by emotions. Our love will be shown by obedience, not by how good we feel about God at a given moment. "And love means following the commands of God. . . ."

"Do you love me?" Jesus asked Peter. "Feed my lambs." He was not asking, "How do you feel about me?" for love is not a feeling. He was asking for action.

We are given the choice, day by day, to choose good and refuse evil. Feelings will not, as a rule, help us very much. Although impulse is not invariably bad, more often than not the choice will be between principle and impulse. What I ought to do and what I feel like doing are seldom the same thing. "The good which I want to do, I fail to do; but what I do is the wrong which is against my will," wrote Paul. This is a disarmingly accurate description of what every Christian experiences. Paul was not happy about it, but he was honest about it—honest enough to put it down on paper. As long as we are in this mortal coil we will experience failure, we will make wrong choices. But the command remains. "Be holy." Let us be honest in recognizing feelings and honest enough to reject them when they are wrong.

> You must therefore be mentally stripped for action, perfectly self-controlled. Fix your hopes on the gift of grace which is to be yours when Jesus Christ is revealed. As obedient children, do not let your characters be shaped any longer by the desires you cherished in your days of ignorance. The One who called you is holy; like him, be holy in all your behaviour. . . .

Later in the same epistle Peter is extremely forthright in telling us exactly what kind of action is called for if we are to be self-controlled and holy:

Abstain from lusts of the flesh
Submit to every human institution for the sake of the Lord
Accept authority

Be one in thought and feeling (impossible if both are not brought under obedience)
Be full of brotherly affection (even if I don't feel like it?)
Be kindly and humble minded
Retaliate with blessing

Not long ago a young woman at a retreat told a long tale of how she had come to know the Lord, had rebelled against Him and gone far afield, had been brought back, rebelled again, and then in mercy and grace the Lord had forgiven her, given her a Christian husband and happiness. He was a highway patrolman, and one day, attending a traffic accident, he was struck by a passing car and critically injured. Gwenn herself was in bed at the time, with a threatened miscarriage. Three days later he died. That same afternoon her father died, and in six more days she lost her baby. She told her story quietly, without tears, although nearly everyone else was weeping. She finished by saying that she found, by her husband's deathbed, what she had sought for so long—the gracious presence of Christ Himself.

In a letter to me she wrote:

About a week after the retreat my phone rang. It was the wife of the man who hit my husband. She said she had to call because her sister-in-law had just called her, having come home from a Bible study where a woman shared some of what I said that morning at the retreat. She literally pleaded with me, if ever the inclination were there, to somehow communicate to her husband the things I had said, because he is so guilt ridden and unable to forgive himself. When I hung up the phone, I was shaking and ran in and fell beside my bed and cried my heart out, knowing, I guess, that such a thing can only be accomplished by God within me—for it's like being stretched far beyond who I am. To hold onto my pain, despising its source, is far easier because it's far more natural. But as a friend said, my forgiving him and expressing that forgiveness directly via a letter or visit could very possibly hold the key, the only key, that can release him from his prison. . . . And it just very well could be the one area I have not dealt with that could result in the completion of healing within me. My friend pointed out that, as a child of God, I really have no choice. The nagging question, "Why, God, is it required of *me* to forgive so much?" needs not be answered. . . . Praise God for His amazing grace that takes us where we never thought we could go!

A few final words of caution:

Do not debunk feelings *as such*. Remember they are given to us as part of our humanity. Do not try to fortify yourself *against* emotions. Recognize them; name them, if that helps; and then lay them open before the Lord for His training of your responses. The discipline of emotions is the training of responses.

No argument for discipline will furnish the power to discipline. He who summons is He who empowers. He is Master. As we give ourselves to His rule He gives us grace to rule.

Saint Francis de Sales put it this way: "We are not masters of our own feeling but we are by God's grace masters of our consent."

Try it. When, in the face of powerful temptation to do wrong, there is the swift, hard renunciation—*I will not*—it will be followed by the sudden loosing of the bonds of self, the yes to God that lets in sunlight, sets us singing and all freedom's bells clanging for joy.

FOURTEEN

Exchange: My Life for His

IT IS MY GREAT DELIGHT these days to watch the growing and learning of a little boy of four and his sister of two. The climate of their home is love, which means that sometimes the sun shines, and sometimes it is cloudy. There is plenty of laughter, story reading, games, popcorn by the fire, cuddling, rocking, and hymn singing. There is also an occasional spanking. A mother and father who love their children cannot allow them to go their own way. They desire for them freedom and joy, things that no fallen human being can find without instruction, example, and correction ("Happy are they who obey his instruction, who set their heart on finding him"). When children surrender gladly to the parents' instructions, it is sunny weather for all. When they refuse, storm clouds gather. The small boy and girl eagerly consent to the suggestion of a story or some popcorn. They are not so eager to pick up toys or eat broccoli. If only the parents could make them see that the purpose in all these things is the children's ultimate happiness and wholeness. They love them enough to say no to most television programs, no to staying up as late as some of their friends, no to junk food. They love them enough to require an hour of solitude and quiet for each child each afternoon. They love them enough to stand by while the children learn to do things by themselves, things the parents are strongly tempted to do for them. They love them enough to allow them, when their growth in wisdom and independence require it, to be hurt, to struggle, and at times, even to fail.

"Is discipline the same as punishment?" a young woman asked me. She was troubled by the idea of God's wanting to "get even." I gave her 1 Corinthians 11:32, NEB, "When ... we do fall under the Lord's judgement, he is disciplining us, to save us from being condemned with the rest of the world." God's "punishment" of his children is never retribution, but rather correction. We know that we are indeed his beloved sons, sharing in the discipline that all sons share—for a high purpose, namely that we may some day share his holiness, "attain life."

The story of Jonah powerfully illustrates the foolishness of saying no to our Father in heaven. Jonah thought he could get out of doing what God asked. Instead of going to Nineveh as commanded, he took ship to Tarshish, thinking he was "out of reach of the Lord." A decision like that is bound to lead to stormy weather of one kind or another, and in Jonah's case it was a literal hurricane. Think what troubles obedience would have saved him from—the storm, the horror of being dumped overboard, the jaws of the great fish looming up from the dim deep, the trauma of finding himself actually swallowed, and three unimaginably dreadful days in the creature's stomach. But it was Inexorable Love that followed him, even into that darkness. It was, in fact, the love of God that ordained that strange means of rescue for His wayward prophet, which the prophet himself came to acknowledge in his prayer from the fish's belly:

> ... Weeds twined about my head
> in the troughs of the mountains;
> I was sinking into a world
> whose bars would hold me fast for ever.

But thou didst bring me up alive from the pit, O Lord
    my God.
As my senses failed me I remembered the Lord,
    and my prayer reached thee in thy holy temple.

Then the Lord spoke to the fish, the fish vomited, and
Jonah was saved. He wasted no time when God gave him a
second chance. "Go to Nineveh." Jonah went at once. Wiser
he was by now, to be sure. How much happier he might have
been if his first response had been that of the psalmist, "Thy
instruction is wonderful; therefore I gladly keep it."

The goal of every true disciple is to please his God. The
Bible is our guidebook, showing us how to do that.

Cooking is a great pleasure for me. I love to cook good
food for people with good appetites. Most of what I do in the
kitchen I do without recipes because it is plain stuff, and I
have done it many times. But once in a great while I have
time to do something wonderful, and I am glad to go to an
authority who can tell me how. If it's a *pâté à choux* that I
need for profiteroles, I don't make up the recipe as I go
along, choosing to throw two cups of flour into boiling water
before I add the butter. It would not be *pâté à choux* in the
end. It would be a mess.

The goal of the cook—a perfect dessert—will not be at-
tained without her first giving up her "right" to do it her
way, then studying the book and doing exactly what it says.
When I am the cook, I surrender easily and happily to a
pastry recipe by M. F. K. Fisher. I take her word for it that if
I do this, I will end up with that.

Why then, instead of taking Christ at His word, do we pre-
fer to argue ("it's too hard, too restrictive, it isn't my thing"),
to claim our "rights," to muddle through on our own? In this
way paradise was lost. It is the same enemy who comes to us

today with the same lie ("you shall not die, but live"). Yet still faithfully Jesus calls to life and to utter bliss those who will follow His way. Granted, it is the way of the cross, but only that way leads to the resurrection.

He offers an exchange: His life for ours. He showed us what He meant by giving Himself. The overwhelming fact of the Son's obedience to the Father—hell itself harrowed by the Infinite Majesty—does it not call us far out of ourselves, far beyond the pitiful, calculating, cowardly, self-serving, self-saving pursuit of what the world calls happiness?

He offers us love, acceptance, forgiveness, a weight of glory, fullness of joy. Is it so hard to offer back the gifts that came in the first place from the wounded hands—body, mind, place, time, possessions, work, feelings?

We have not, of course, exhausted the list of things to be surrendered. We have included only a sampling as an aid to perceiving the principle of self-offering that works this way:

If we suffer with Christ, we will reign with Him

If a grain of wheat dies, it produces fruit

If we relinquish our mourning, God gives us a garment of praise

If we bring our sins, He replaces them with a robe of righteousness

Joy comes not in spite of, but because of, sorrow

When discipline becomes a glad surrender, "Every day we experience something of the death of Jesus, so that we may also know the power of the life of Jesus in these bodies of ours."

Source Notes

Source Notes

Chapter 6

P. T. Forsyth, *The Principle of Authority* (London: Hodder & Stoughton, n.d.), p. 404, *italics added.*	34
Genesis 6:13, 14, 18 RSV	36
James 2:17 NEB	36
Hebrews 11:7 NEB	36
2 Corinthians 5:19 NEB	39
Philippians 3:8 YOUNG CHURCHES	39
John 1:12 NEB, *italics added*	40
1 Peter 1:5 NEB	40
Hebrews 4:2 NEB	40
John 1:13 RSV	40
Romans 9:16 NEB	40
John 8:31, 32, *italics added*	40
Psalms 119:75 RSV	41
2 Thessalonians 1:5, 11 NEB	41
Judges 6:36 NEB, *italics added*	42
Nehemiah 4:9 NEB, *italics added*	42
Nehemiah 5:16; 6:16 NEB, *italics added*	42
1 Peter 5:6 NEB, *italics added*	42
2 Chronicles 10:15 NEB	42
Acts 4:28 NEB	42
Genesis 50:20 NEB	42
Mark 14:21 NEB	42
Acts 2:23 NEB	42

Chapter 7

Hebrews 12:14 NEB	44
1 Thessalonians 4:3–5, 7 NEB	44, 45
Romans 12:1 margin NEB	45
Romans 12:1 JERUSALEM	45
Philippians 3:21 NEB	46
Romans 6:6 KJV	46
Romans 8:10 KJV	46
1 Corinthians 6:15 KJV	46
Daniel 1:9 NEB	46, 47
Acts 13:3 NEB	49
Acts 14:23 NEB	49
Matthew 25:31–46	49
Matthew 6:18 NEB	49
Henry Twells, "At Even, When the Sun Was Set" *Episcopal Hymnal* (N.Y.: Seabury Press, 1943).	50
Deuteronomy 21:20 RSV	50
1 Corinthians 6:20 NEB	52
1 Corinthians 9:27 PHILLIPS	53
1 Timothy 4:8 NEB	53
1 Corinthians 6:13 YOUNG CHURCHES	54
Malcolm Muggeridge, entry for March 26, 27, 1951, *Diaries* (London: Collins, 1981).	55
John Donne, *The John Donne Treasury,* ed. Erwin P. Rudolph (Wheaton, Ill.: Victor Books, 1978), p. 85.	55,56
1 Corinthians 15:44 NEB	56
"Whistled" for, Zechariah 10:8 NEB	56

Chapter 8

1 Peter 1:13 NEB 57
Matthew 22:37 NEB, *italics added* 57
Romans 12:1 NEB, *italics added* 57
Romans 12:3 NEB 59
Colossians 3:2 60
Ephesians 1:17, 20 NEB 60
C. S. Lewis, *A Preface to Paradise Lost* (N.Y.:
    Oxford University Press, 1942). 62
1 John 1:18 NEB 62
François de Fénelon, *Spiritual Letters to Women*
    (New Canaan, Conn.: Keats Publishing Co.). 62, 63
John 7:7 NEB 63
John 15:18–20 NEB 63
Colossians 3:2 64
F. W. H. Meyers, *Saint Paul* (London: H. R. Allenson,
    Ltd, n.d.). 64
Kate B. Wilkinson, "May the Mind of Christ My Savior." 65
1 Corinthians 2:2, 3 NEB 65
Romans 12:2 JERUSALEM 66
Proverbs 15:32 NEB 67
Ephesians 6:12, 13 PHILLIPS 68, 69
2 Corinthians 10:3–5 NEB 69
From a sermon by Dr. Charles Stanley, In Touch
    Ministries, Box 7900, Atlanta, Ga. 30357, #AQ031,
    used by permission. 69
1 Timothy 6:3–5 NEB 70
See also Elisabeth Elliot, *Let Me Be a Woman*
    (Wheaton, Ill.: Tyndale House, 1976) and *The Mark
    of a Man* (Old Tappan, N.J.: Fleming H. Revell,
    1981). 72
Psalms 119:33–37 NEB 72, 73
Titus 1:10, 11, 16 NEB 73, 74
Hebrews 4:12, 13 NEB 74
1 Corinthians 14:33 KJV 75
Psalms 32:8–11 NEB 75
Psalms 18:28, 30 NEB 76
James 3:15, 17 NEB 78
John 6:67, 68 NEB 79

Chapter 9

1 Peter 2:17 NEB 80
Romans 13:7, 8 NEB 81
Acts 10:34 KJV 81
James 2:3 81
Matthew 22:11–14 82
1 Peter 2:17 NEB 83
Romans 12:10 NEB 84
Isak Dinesen, *Out of Africa* (N.Y.: Random House,
    1972), p. 261. 84
Luke 6:28, 30 NEB 85
Leviticus 19:15, 16 NEB 85
1 Timothy 5:17 KJV 86
1 Timothy 5:17 NEB 86
Philippians 2:30 NEB 86

Source Notes

Chapter 12
Luke 3:13, 14 NEB   122
Dag Hammarskjöld, *Markings* (London:
    Faber & Faber, 1975), p. 109.   123
2 Corinthians 10:13–15 YOUNG CHURCHES   125
Acts 6:3 NEB   126
Psalms 24:3, 4 KJV   128
Ecclesiastes 12:12 RSV   129
Psalms 90:17 KJV   130
Colossians 3:22–24 NEB   132
Exodus 35:30–36:1 NEB   134
2 Thessalonians 3:8–12 NEB   136
Hebrews 6:12 NEB   137

Chapter 13
Luke 14:16–20   138
Daniel 6:20, 23 NEB   139
Daniel 7:15, 28; 8:15, 17, 27 NEB   139
George MacDonald, *Unspoken Sermons* (London:
    Longman's, Green & Co., 1906).   139
Daniel 10:1, 8–12, 15 NEB   140
Alexander Schmemann, *Church, World, Mission*
    (Crestwood, N.Y.: St. Vladimir's, 1979), p. 124.   141, 142
Nehemiah 5:6, 7, 9 NEB   142
Acts 14:15 NEB   143
James 5:17 NEB   143
Isaiah 50:7 NEB   143
Saint John of the Cross, *Councils of Light and Love*
    (N.Y.: Paulist Press, 1977).   143
Jude 4 YOUNG CHURCHES   144
Romans 8:7 NEB   144
Galatians 5:17 NEB   144
1 Samuel 15:23 NEB   145
Titus 3:3 NEB   145
Romans 8:12, 13 YOUNG CHURCHES   145
Philippians 3:1 YOUNG CHURCHES   146
Romans 12:8 NEB   146
2 Kings 18:5, 7   146
Galatians 5:22 NEB   146
Romans 4:25 NEB   148
Jude 19   148
2 John 6 NEB   148
Romans 7:19 NEB   149
1 Peter 1:13–15 NEB   149

Chapter 14
Psalms 119:2 NEB   152
Hebrews 12:9 NEB   153
Jonah 2:5, 7 NEB   153, 154
Psalms 119:129 NEB   154
2 Corinthians 4:10 PHILLIPS   155